Through the eyes of a youngster

Through the eyes of a youngster

The Christmas Tree
1947

W. Meyer

Illustrations by F. Meyer

ISBN-13: 9781545242285
ISBN-10: 1545242283

This book is a book of love.

I have written all these stories for my children and grandchildren, wife, brothers, nephews, nieces, aunts and uncles, all the in-laws and dear friends so that they may know the adventures I had as a small boy living in Germany during and right after the second world war.

It was so very different from life as it is nowadays.

I would very much like to thank my dear wife for doing all the illustrations, typing, etc. and to my daughter for all the hard work as my editor. And specially for having so much patience with me!

Author's note:
All the events described in this book actually happened as I remember but all names of people have been changed to protect their identities.

CONTENTS

Through the eyes of

a youngster

CHAPTER 1

THROUGH THE EYES OF A YOUNGSTER

We lived in a very small town near the Munich-Salzburg autobahn, a little west of the jewel like setting of the Chiemsee Lake and a little north of the alpine mountains.

It was 1946. The war had been over for a year. We lived in the American military zone. Less than 100 km to the east, the Russian military occupied Austria.

Our onion topped village church was 2 km up the hill, northwest from our house, about half an hours' brisk walk. To get there we either had to cross over the autobahn on a long bridge or under it on a farm path beside the Auer creek.

From this long bridge we had the best views of the huge amount of military equipment and vehicles that rumbled towards Salzburg or Munich. The trucks fascinated us, especially those with 3 axles, where one set could be pulled up and could load tanks, jeeps and mobile canons. The tanks vibrated the ground and we could feel the vibrations up on the overpass.

Some days were quiet and hardly anyone was on the Autobahn. One day, we could hear a revving engine far away. Then, two soldiers on belt driven motorcycles - one a JAP and the other a Harley, went speeding by. A few minutes later, an open military police jeep, with two soldiers wearing white helmets, zoomed by trying to catch up to the motorbikes. My brother Rudi explained to us younger brothers that the autobahn was ideal for racing.

Refugees from all parts of Eastern Europe found shelter in our village. These were rough and hard times. We learned to barter and trade for anything that was edible.

My parent's home was a small farmhouse with five rooms and a kitchen. Our family consisted of eight people, three adults and five boys. Mr. and Mrs. Prixel and their daughter Sarah also lived with us. They were refugees from Hungary. Mr. Prixel had been a German language teacher at the University of Budapest. They now lived in one room. It was the biggest room in our house, the one with the large bay window. They had a small wood stove in one corner, a small table with two chairs on the same side as their beds, and a small cabinet.

Dad added a small room to his workshop so that his helper could live there. He was a shifty, fearsome character that no one trusted. Our Mother did not like him. She always could sense if a person had a bad character or had something to hide. Later we found out through other people what a bad man he really was. His name was Ertl Wacker.

The neighbor's house to the northwest was called "the Baron's" because the former owner had had a Baron title. It was very common in this area for the houses to have different names than their present owners. For instance, the Shuster's farm was occupied by the Steiner family, and the Hemper farm by the Fisher family. Some old farmhouses had their names for hundreds of years. The Baron's had a boy my age named Wolfgang and a younger girl called Clara. We spent a lot of time with them and they were an important part of our childhood group. The Baron's house was a bigger house. They were blessed with an addition of three refugee families.

Next door to the Baron's was "the Administration House". The director of the brick factory had lived there when the factory was in operation prior to 1912, and thus the name. The Pichler family was the present owner. Their family consisted of Opa, Oma, and their daughter Anna, and her son Alois, who was my age and a great play companion. They also had three refugee families that lived with them. The refugee family that settled on the ground floor was the Koehler family. On the first floor were Mrs. Kosak and her two little girls, Erika and Susana, who were a bit younger than us. The Madina family lived in the attic. Most refugee families consisted of grandparents, mothers and children. Most fathers were either fallen, missing in action or in war prison camps in Russia. It was terribly sad.

Refugee families generally lived in a separate room and each had a small stove to cook on. Most of these houses had only one bathroom per floor that they all had to share. These people were very poor and there was never enough to eat.

These families eventually had a few cages with rabbits that were raised to ensure some meat supply. As children, we were very busy collecting "sharling", a broad leaf plant that the rabbits loved to munch on. The smell of these rabbit cages was extremely strong even though they were cleaned out daily.

Albert Madina was only thirteen years old, yet we considered him a grown up. He had a tiny little knife, which he used to carve small swallows, small skis with boots on them and other ornaments, which he sold or traded. People liked to wear them as decorations for their hats.

Winters in our region were always very cold. Everybody collected dry wood from the surrounding forest to heat our homes. As children, we always picked up dry sticks and branches to take home with us. We did this automatically.

In May, the fruit trees bloomed. This was important for us because we could tell by the amount of blossoms, how much fruit we could expect to have later in the summer. We knew every wild apple, cherry or nut tree, including beechnut within a 4 km radius. When the Linden trees bloomed, everyone harvested as many blossoms as they could so that it could be dried and made into tea. It tasted mild and sweet almost like honeysuckle. Everyone enjoyed it.

This year, we noticed that the crows were very active and that they were building nests. Opa Koehler coaxed us to observe these crows more closely, as they were a delicacy to eat. Crows are very smart. They sensed that they were being watched, so they did not fly directly to their nest. They stopped here and there, and eventually flew to their nest in a round about way. After the eggs hatched, the crows started feeding their young. As they got bigger, the babies demanded more food. Crows raided other bird nests. They grabbed baby chickens, ducklings and whatever else they could get hold of. We told Opa Koehler that we knew the whereabouts of at least a dozen nests with their young. We climbed neighboring trees to see the crow's nests and how the young were growing. The crows always managed to build their nests in the tallest fir trees. Opa told us to wait one more week. This week passed very quickly.

Finally, it was time for my brother and I to climb up one of the trees where there was a crows' nest. It was pandemonium! The wind was blowing, the trees were swaying and the crows attacked. We were scared! The crows defended their young by screeching and dive-bombing us. We were very afraid that the crows might peck our eyes out. We only had one arm to defend ourselves as we were hanging on to the tree for dear life. We emptied three more nests that day and put the young crows in an old burlap sack.

We ran to Opa Koehler's place with the birds. He was so delighted he danced a jig and sang a song in a language we did not understand. He grabbed the birds and very quickly went over to his wood chopping block, chopped their heads off, plucked off the feathers and gutted them. They were ready for the roasting pan. This catch became a delicious feast of roasted "doves" for everyone that lived in his house much to the delight of the refugee families. And in Opa Koehler's eyes we sure were heroes!

In 1946 and thereafter we raided quite a lot of crow nests.

The Creek Running by Our House

CHAPTER 2

THE CREEK RUNNING BY OUR HOUSE

The creek by our house was called the Ache and IT was our playground. We spent hours playing in and around it. In the summer, when it was super hot, we cooled off down by the creek. Even when the water was very low, it was cold as it was snowmelt from the nearby mountains.

We looked for stones with beautiful colors and patterns. Sometimes, very fine grey-blue tile clay became exposed. We loved this stuff. It was great to play with. The clay was perfect to create little animals, like giant ladybugs, salamanders, little boys and girls, cats, etc. We used pebbles for eyes and we scratched in whiskers and other details with tiny slivers of wood. We created with limitless imaginations!

Mom of course, was never too pleased when we tried baking our clay art products in the kitchen wood stove. None of the creatures ever dried properly and always cracked and crumbled when baked thus leaving a mess in her roasting oven.

We loved to redirect shallow water flows. We became experts in making water wheels. Not far from our house, there was a small waterfall. It was easy to put a waterwheel under it. We put nails on either side of the wheel, which became the cogs. On every turn, the cogs pushed down the arm of a wooden hammer, which in turn banged on an old pot, can or tin lid. These made great sounds… the beginnings of melodies. Many times, Dad got angry with us when we left some of his best tools down by the creek. When the snow melted in the surrounding mountains, we had high water in the creek, and all of our waterwheels were swept away by the current.

Sometimes, when there was heavy rain in the mountains, the water rose in the creek. The force of the floodwater often destroyed Dad's weir and filled it with gravel. (A **weir** is a barrier across a river, smaller than a dam, pooling water behind them while also allowing it to flow steadily over their tops.) When the creek flooded, our land was completely under water. Of course, it did this in the middle of the night. Mom said that "it always flooded after midnight." The water flooded our cellar under our house on more than one occasion. The floor of Dad's workshop was made out of large wooden blocks, and when the water rushed in all the blocks that the machines were not directly sitting on, floated in thirty centimeters of water and the machines shifted… It was a mess.

After the floods, it was always hard work cleaning up and shoveling all the gravel out of the weir. The whole family stood bare foot in the water and together, we dug it out.

The creek was always our treasured playground.

The War was On - 1944-45

CHAPTER 3

THE WAR WAS ON! - 1944/45

Allied forces bomber squadrons flew daily missions into Germany from their bases near Milano, Italy. Quite a number of them swerved east in order to avoid flying their direct route to Munich to avoid being predictable for the anti-aircraft gunnery stations that were waiting for them. This route brought them into Germany over the Alps, close to where we lived.

You could hear the hard working motors of the heavy bombers well before you could see them, usually at the same time that the air attack siren started wailing. We called it the rumbling thunder, as this is what the airplane engines sounded like. The high pitch siren carried really far depending on the wind and weather, all the way from Rosenheim. It was very scary for us when the sirens went off because this could mean the end of our lives.

To defeat the German radar system of the anti-aircraft gun batteries, the Allied planes dropped aluminum tinsel in small bundles. This sent false reading back to the Germans. As children we looked for and found these tinsel bundles. They were our trophies!

Mom made emergency packsacks for everyone in the family. Each were stuffed with extra winter clothes and a package of twice baked, very hard dry bread. When the siren wailed, we had to move fast. We grabbed our packsacks and ran out of the house, towards the creek. We crossed over the creek on a very long and heavy wooden plank. Then we continued running up the wooded ravine to the bomb shelter that Opa had dug out for us.

The shelter was a simple square hole in the ground. The entrance tunnel went into the ravine horizontally, on one side of a big oak tree. Inside, the earth was supported with heavy timber. Once in the shelter, we sat on a wooden bench and waited until the sirens stopped screaming. While we waited, Opa prayed aloud: "Holy Mary, protect us. Lift up your arms and make a shelter and an umbrella for us. Let this tragic moment pass." He prayed sincerely and we all joined in.

Many of the air attacks were at night, just after dusk or in the shelter of the clouds. There were anti-aircraft guns close to our house because we could see their searchlights from our shelter. In the lights, you could see the planes. They were very small, but shiny and silvery, while everything else was pitch black. Once the searchlights found the planes, we could see the tracer bullets the anti-aircraft guns plowed into the sky. Most of them did not hit the targeted planes. If the wind picked up, it muffled the shooting sounds.

About fifteen to twenty minutes after we first heard the planes, they would reach Munich. The planes dropped flares that brightly lit up the skies over the city for a long time as they were attached to multiple parachutes. Then we would hear the terrifying sounds of bombs exploding all over Munich. Opa had lost his home in Munich to bombing and was now living with us.

Opa suspected that in order to get back over the mountains, bombers that had lost engines or had any engine trouble had to eject any extra weight. Also, planes wanting to travel at higher altitudes had to ditch extra weight. Bombers had extra fuel tanks attached to their wings that they could drop on their return flights. Planes also did not want to be hit with bombs on board on their return flight, as they could explode. They also had to ditch any bombs that got stuck in their bomb bays. When they dropped bombs, they dropped many at a time, releasing one after the other. Sometimes, the release mechanism did not release all of them and some were inadvertently left on board.

Consequently, as we lived near the Alps, they dropped bombs all around our farmhouse. They left craters all over the fields and the forest. As the craters filled up with ground or rainwater, they became very dangerous. In our area, we had lots of blue clay under the topsoil. This blue clay was very slippery and made it extremely difficult to climb out of a crater when you fell in. Many animals drowned when they slid in and they could not climb out. Our Mom warned us many times not to go near these dangerous craters.

We were out in the countryside when our neighbor's house got a hit. Luckily, the owners were not in at the time.

One day, Opa screamed "Bomber coming!" This was very strange because the airplane was flying at a very low altitude and was coming from Munich. We ran to our shelter and were there within minutes. Sure enough, Opa saw an object falling from the airplane towards our property. Then we heard snapping of big branches and a loud ssrrppff. At the same time, the birds stopped chirping and there was dead silence all around us. I could hear my heart thumping in my chest! Everyone was still…

Opa told us to lie down, to plug our ears with our fingers to prevent pressure wave damage and then to wait for the explosion, but nothing happened for a very long time. It was probably only about 5 minutes, but it felt like forever. Then, Opa ordered us to stay in the shelter while he went to investigate. Very slowly and carefully, he went in the opposite direction of where the sound came from so he would have a better view of the impact spot. Once he could see that it was safe, he whistled for us to come out.

We ran to Opa and he warned us not to get too close. There was a huge, metal, auxiliary gas tank, pointy on both ends, stuck in between a bunch of trees. Pink fluid was slowly leaking out of a hole. Opa said that it smells like benzene (aircraft gasoline) but that it did not look like it. He told us to go and fetch some containers as fast as we could. All of us children ran - some of us back to our home and others to the neighbors. We brought back gas cans, buckets, and every kind of odd container that we could find. We filled up whatever we could. We ended up with about 30 liters of premium USA octane gasoline. The German people had never seen pink fuel before, as theirs was clear like water. We shared the fuel equally with the neighbors who had helped us collect it. It became a very sought after commodity that we used to barter for food.

After the war ended, the older boys from the neighborhood retrieved the auxiliary tank that had fallen from the sky. They cut a big hole out in the middle so that someone could sit in it and paddle with it like a kayak. They took it to a nearby fishing pond and tested it. However, one of the dare devil boys flipped it over and nearly drowned because he had a hard time getting out. This scared us little guys and we did not even want to look at it again.

Many, many years later I sold the gas tank as scrap metal!

American Troops

1945

CHAPTER 4

AMERICAN TROOPS

At about noon on a winter day, American troops stopped on a field beside the autobahn, on the north side, heading in the direction of Salzburg-Munich. Our house was about 700 meters downhill, in the valley.

It was a very cold and the snow was knee deep. The first thing the soldiers did, was build a huge bonfire. They cut down a bunch of trees close by for firewood. The Americans were experts at chopping wood and building fires. They poured a lot of gasoline over the piled up wood and started the fire. At first, the flames rose higher than a house, like a fireball that we could see from far away. We guessed that the troops must have decided to have their lunch break and warm up by a fire.

After a while, we heard some gunshots, which echoed loudly against the local hills. What was going on? We were baffled. It did not sound like target practice. As quickly as the gunshots started, they stopped and it was quiet again.

Two hours later, we heard motors revving up. The American troops packed up and left, driving towards

Munich. They left the fire embers burning. The older refugee children like Albert Madina and Roland Koepler (who were twelve years old) were the first to check out the bonfire spot. They found about twenty-four empty, shinny gun shells. They were really happy to find these trophies to play with and to show off. They quickly put a lot of snow on the embers to douse the fire and save the remaining wood. Wood was very valuable so they dragged it back to their homes as fast as they could.

Opa was interested in what the American troops had shot at. He arrived at the bonfire site and started to investigate. He walked across the field to the far side of the meadow. By this time, all the immediate neighbors arrived at this spot as well. Everyone was very curious as to what had happened.

Sure enough, Opa found deer tracks. He knew in which direction the deer was running by the footprints left in the snow. He followed them, and after a while, found some blood drops. Opa continued to follow the deer tracks for another kilometer. It looked like the deer had escaped into some underbrush, but it was getting dark, so he had to stop the search.

In the meantime, all the children searched for loot and treasures. The younger children found orange peels in the snow. They generously divided the peels so that each child could have a taste. These orange peels were thoroughly enjoyed, as the children had never tasted anything similar before.

That evening the three old men in the neighborhood had tea together in our kitchen. Us children were not included in the meeting, so we stretched our ears to hear what was being said. We really wanted to know what they were talking about, but at the same time, we could guess that they were talking about the deer tracks.

Early the next day, all the children were officially informed that their help was needed, which made us all feel very important. We were asked to search in the underbrush for any sign of the deer. It was easier if we searched the underbrush, instead of the old folks going down on their hands and knees to crawl in the snow. We spread out and searched the underbrush from the top of the hill on down.

After about one hour and a half of searching, Albert Madina found the deer, dead under a cluster of young spruce trees. We all helped to drag the deer out. Very secretly and quickly, we put the deer on a sleigh, covered it with a tarp and brought it home. We made sure that no one, outside the three-neighbor circle, had any idea of what was going on otherwise there would have been too many people claiming part of the meat!

Opa got busy butchering the deer. He prepared the meat and divided it into equal portions. Nothing was wasted. It was my chore to tell the two neighboring houses, with all the refugee families living there, to bring a pot and collect their share. When the people collected their deer meat including the fat and bones they were very happy and thanked Opa profusely for the work he had done. I could see that Opa was a hero!

Guess what we had on the dinner table that night? Yes, you guessed right! We had the most delicious deer stew. Opa thanked the Lord for providing us with love for each other and the wonderful stew. He also thanked the Lord that he let us have the deer meat instead of the army soldiers. They could not have needed it as much as the refugees. Opa said that it was heaven sent. Mom was the first to agree with him.

At one time in his younger years Opa had worked in a butcher shop in Munich. He knew how to butcher and prepare the meat. It was an easy job for him to do. He also knew how to cure leather. Many months later he prepared the hide of the deer up in the attic of Dad's workshop. He was able to make six pairs of leather gloves and two pairs of slippers (house shoes) from the deer and still had bits of leather left over.

Escargot

CHAPTER 5

ESCARGOT

In post war Germany, people were hungry and undernourished. The store shelves were empty and food rationing was in effect. Food rationing meant that you could only buy food that you had food stamps for. Each person was only entitled to monthly food stamps for 250 grams of meat, 400 grams of flour, 2 kilograms of potatoes and 100 grams of sugar. Although you received a stamp for sugar, there just wasn't any. The food rations left people desperate to find whatever else they could to eat to supplement their daily nutrition. These were desperate times.

The stores carried next to nothing. Whenever a shipment came in, word spread like wildfire, and everyone went quickly to the store to pick up as much of their rationing as possible. Whatever came into the store was usually sold out within the hour.

Many people planted vegetable gardens. Homeowners designated little garden plots for the refugees living in their houses. The government also allocated small plots of land, that were not being used for anything else, to be gardened. As gardens were so small, everyone was always striving to get the most out of their plots. This led to competition - who could grow the most, or the biggest vegetables. People were proud to show off what they were able to grow, through their hard labor and their ingenuities. They were very resourceful and made things like fences by weaving willow branches, to keep the wild hares out.

As we walked to school, we walked by many gardens. We talked to the people tending their plots. Sometimes they would share a small sample of their produce, like a pea or bean pod. Gardens were tended with lots of love and attention. Work was done to keep the weeds out, catch the mice, get rid of the moles, keep wild rabbits out, and to prevent the butterflies from laying eggs in the cabbage plants. Very early in the morning plants were watered by hand.

The most important crop was the potato and then root vegetables such as carrots, beets, kohlrabi, and turnips. Other popular vegetables that were grown were kidney beans, cabbage for sauerkraut, onions and tomatoes. The celery root was a much-desired vegetable because it was perfect for soups, sauces and salads.

People collected wild edibles. In the springtime, we collected young dandelion leaves for salads. We also collected young stinging nettles. The leaves were delicious, similar to spinach - steamed of course! However, harvesting them was a different matter. The young leaves do not have the prickles that the mature ones do. If you were not careful, you could get stung on your hands, arms and sometimes on your legs too. Stings caused a horrible, very itchy, red rash. We learnt very quickly and did not let the nettles sting us.

Quite a few people raised rabbits in cages behind their houses. They were easy to grow, good to eat and a good source of protein. People sold them privately or traded them for other things.

At the edge of meadows, there were always lots of slugs and snails. We boys collected the snails. They were quite big, often the size of a baby's fist. The snails would glide along their slimy trails, with their houses on their backs. But, when you picked them up, they would retreat into their shells. Our mom did not like them and was quite disgusted when we brought some into our house for her to cook!

Grandma Madina, who lived across the street, knew how to cook these snails. We collected 2 big buckets full of snails and delivered them to her. She put them into a burlap sack, salted them, tied a knot at the top, and hung the sack on to a tree branch overnight. The snails expelled lots of slime through the burlap sack. By the next morning, they were ready. Grandma Madina washed them in a huge glass bowl with lots of fresh water. Then, she put them in a big pot with a bit of water, garlic and local herbs. In no time at all, they were ready. She served them with boiled potatoes.

The residents in the house where she lived were invited to partake in this feast of escargot. They smelled good, but I wasn't going to taste them. My bigger brother Hans, on the other hand, was a daring boy. He ate two of them and told me that they tasted like candy… but I wasn't fooled. Besides, how would he have known what candies tasted like? There were no candies in all of the land, so he teased me. And I knew better.

From then on, many a bucket of snails were delivered with love, from us boys to Grandma Madina, who was truly thankful and enjoyed every feast that she shared with her neighbors.

Mushroom Harvest

CHAPTER 6

MUSHROOM HARVEST

It was common for families to go on long hikes on mountain trails or around nearby lakes. After the church service, on the second Sunday of September, Dad recommended that we go and check out our secret boletus spots and look for other mushrooms. There were some high clouds in the sky and a gentle breeze. Sunshine seemed to be promised for the rest of the day. It would be pleasant and warm, a perfect day for a September hike.

"Be alert for anything," Dad advised us five boys. "Maybe we have a chance to see a deer or a fox in the forest and be especially careful not to step on any sharp objects or broken glass. Most of all, don't step into wasps nests that are in the ground." We all nodded in agreement as we all had been walking around barefoot since the end of April. By this time in the year, we all had had our share of thorns, splinters, cuts, wasps and nettle sting so our feet were well conditioned. We would not be wearing our shoes again until the middle of October, weather permitting. He also told us that whoever finds the biggest boletus will be the "Mushroom King"…until a bigger one is found.

There were about ten different kinds of edible mushrooms growing in our area. The best and the most desired were the boletus. The others mushrooms had different shapes and flavors, and had a definite order of preference. They were all compared against the boletus.

We followed Dad. He carried a four-gallon wicker basket in which he had a light vest, a small knife, and a ten-foot light hemp rope. Dad always had a strong string or rope with him as part of the essential items needed to be out in the woods.

In single file, we crossed the creek at a narrow spot, over a fallen tree. Then we hiked up hill and crossed a meadow where we entered the forest. Once we were in the forest, it was colder. We automatically separated; three boys went to the left, and two to the right of Dad in order to spread out and search for mushrooms. Rudi and Hans found the first family of boletus. They carefully extracted them from the forest soil and handed them over to Dad for inspection. They were all healthy and went in the basket. Before putting these mushrooms in the basket, Dad cut off a very small piece off the bottom part of the stem that had to be put back where they grew as these spores became the seeds for the next crop.

As we were walking, we spotted a poisonous mushroom that had been kicked over. Dad said, "This is a sign that Isaac Sr. was here two days ago. He couldn't be very smart because he has the habit of kicking over poisonous mushrooms and leaving a trail behind him. Anyone can follow where he has been and find any of his secret mushroom spots."

The mushroom locations were always kept top secret. No one would volunteer any information as to their whereabouts. However, most residents had their preferred spots, but also knew when others had been on the same trail. Our Dad made an extra effort to teach us boys to be quiet and careful not to leave any trace behind us.

When we arrived at the bend of our creek, the water level was not high. We could just walk across it barefoot, but Dad had to take his shoes off to get across! Dad showed us where the creek had washed away soil and exposed a thick black layer in the ground, about two and a half meters deep. He told us that people hundreds of years ago made charcoal by burning wood in pits and covering it to reduce their oxygen, a process that took days. Deep soil is needed for this, and soft soil is usually found along the banks of creeks. If you touched the black soil, it made your hands black. People in the village used this black earth. Some used it to top off their geranium boxes that decorated their balconies and windows. Others used it to top off the earth at the base of their rose bushes.

From the charcoal, we went up a gentle incline and found a spot with lots of different kinds of mushrooms, including a bonus of half a dozen boletuses. The bottom of Dad's basket started to fill up. On our way to the next stop we crossed an area with a bit more undergrowth. Suddenly, Dad stopped and pointed up a tree. That was a signal for us to stop and also look up. A large brown owl sat on a lower branch of a tall spruce tree. It looked at us with its big bright eyes and chirped once. Then, it turned its head around, as if it had no neck bone in its body. Dad whispered to us that this owl was almost sleeping, but at sundown, it would hunt mice all night long.

Shortly after we saw a mushroom that had been thrown against an old tree and part of it was stuck on the bark at eye level. The rest of it had fallen on the ground. "You see boys," Dad whispered, "Ignatius Zossner did this. He found a mushroom that was wormy. It made him so mad that he flung the mushroom against the tree and left a trail behind. What a noodle head he is!"

As we continued on, we passed by a huge granite stone, standing mysteriously in the forest. It had the number MCCCXVI (1316) carved in it and a coat of arms below. This stone marker was fifty centimeters square, as tall as a man, and had a pointy tip on the top. Dad explained to us that this was a boundary marker, marking the property belonging to the Bishop of Salzburg that had been erected in the year 1316. "A lot of ghosts must be dancing around this one at night," he told us. We thought that this was very funny because there was a lot of small undergrowth at the base of the marker and absolutely no footprints., But then again, ghosts float, and therefore don't trample anything or leave trails behind them.

We had to cross the creek again, as the creek wound its way down into the valley. Hans and Rudi could not resist trying to catch a trout by hand, but this particular spot had a very deep area that the trouts escaped to.

To get to the next mushroom spot we followed a deer trail. We noticed that there were some green leaves curled up every so often and then a small branch lying on the ground. This repeated itself every so often. We became very curious, so we asked Dad what the significance of this was. We knew that deer or hare did not do this.

"No, no" Dad said. "Mr. and Mrs. Cundle were here. Mrs. Cundle has the habit of breaking off small branches of the underbrush then she plucks off the leaves, one at a time, checking to see if her husband loves her or not. If she ends up with a not, she flings the bare branch away and breaks off a new one and starts all over again. So you see boys, she left a trail behind and she is prob- ably not sure whether her husband loves her or not! They were here four days ago."

Hans said to Dad "Okay, we know now that they too left a trail behind but how can you be so sure that they were here four days ago?" Dad answered. "This is very simple. The leaves on the trail are all curled up and that is a result of having no moisture in to them. It takes about 4 days to become so dry."

Finally, we arrived at the spot that was furthest away from home on our quest. My younger brother Franz and I found three very big healthy boletuses.

"WOW!" We claimed our title of "Mushroom Kings" immediately before we even extracted them from the ground. Dad was very pleased with us and put them very carefully on one side of his wicker basket. After that, we found three more, but they were not as large. When Dad inspected these ones, he found that they were all wormy so Dad put down his wicker basket and replanted them very carefully in the moss about thirty feet away and slightly uphill. He explained that if someone comes along, the new mushrooms would lead him or her away from our best spot.

As we walked towards home, a hare startled us when it jumped out from behind a nearby tree and ran away. Franz and I immediately went to the hare's hideout. It seemed to be a very comfortable spot at the base of a tree trunk, nicely sheltered from the West wind and rain and the spruce needles were soft and dry for him to sleep on. We were sure that Mr. Hare would come back to this place again. Dad told us that a hare like this one probably has a dozen spots where he sleeps. "Actually," he said, "hares never sleep. They are always on guard, with their ears standing up and their eyes open. To survive, they have to be smarter, faster, and much more alert then their enemies the fox, the hawk or the eagle."

Next we found a new mushroom spot just off the trail. There were lots of boletus and others of good quality. We collected all of them after Dad inspected them.

Further south, we noticed that someone must have hit a mushroom with a stick – like playing hockey with it. The fungus was divided into a thousand little pieces and was spread over a large area on the moss. Dad said, "It was Tomas Wimper who did this. He always walks with a stick but he does not need one. When he sees a poisonous mushroom, he hits it with his stick. He does not realize that by doing this, he multiplies them for the coming year. He is another person who can't go through the forest without leaving a trail behind him. The wild animals must be laughing at him."

We then walked along the creek on the deer trail. To the right the slope continued uphill but not very steeply. Here Anton, Hans and Rudi discovered a nice group of mushrooms and a hatful of cantharellus mushrooms. A little further on up the hill we also found a fox den in the ground, right beside a tree. It looked as if the fox had worked very hard to dig out the soil. We looked into it but could not see anything.

"THE FOX!" Dad yelled. We all jumped back. Our imaginations had the fox charging out of the den and coming right at us. Dad laughed so hard! He had tricked us good. He then told us that most fox dens have more than one exit. We looked around but could not find anything. We suspected that maybe the fox family had not finished digging it or maybe they had abandoned it. There were many paw prints in the dried mud outside the den.

On our walks, we usually encountered wildlife. We came to a clearing and heard a loud and fast knocking "rrrrttttrtrt, rrrrttttrtrtr." We walked very quietly towards the sound. There, high up in the tree, was a red headed woodpecker. He was busy chipping out rotten wood to get at the ants. The tree had been hit by lightning years before, which had left the tree damaged and rotting. We watched the woodpecker chisel and hammer away at the tree while we took a deserved rest.

As we walked along the clearing, Dad covered his wicker basket with his vest. We wondered why he did this. We found out soon enough. Way down on the other side of the clearing, Isaac walked toward us. When we reached him we exchanged greetings. Isaac eyed Dad's basket and asked my father "Tony, did you find lots of mushrooms?" Dad replied, "Oh! A few, but we are still looking for the big boletus." Isaac wished us good luck and a nice day before going on his way.

At the edge of the forest, there was a giant anthill, about a meter high and a meter wide. This was very interesting for us to see. All those ants working so hard carrying spruce needles to make their anthill higher. They carried broken leaves to feed their young ones.

Dad told us that these ants were also meat eaters. He said that one time, a farmer threw a dead snake onto the anthill, and a few days later, only a white, clean skeleton remained on top of the anthill. Hans then asked Dad if the snake had been a poisonous one. From then on we walked carefully, and watched our bare feet.

There were lots of spruce cones that were all torn apart on the trail, evidence that squirrels had been busy harvesting seeds. Close to the top of a tree, a hawk family had made their nest. One hawk was always circling high above the meadow.

When we arrived at a fork in the trail, we decided to take the shorter route through the woods to continue looking for mushrooms.

Dad got something in his shoe that hurt his foot, so he sat down on a tree stump and took his shoe off. He searched his sock for the prickle that bothered him. While he sat, Dad told us the story of the two pilgrims Bartholomy and Aloisious.

"Bartholomy and Aloisious both drank too much beer at a wedding party and made a nuisance of themselves. The local priest, Father Martinus, told them that if they wanted to be absolved of their misbehavior, they would have to make a pilgrimage to Altoetting, which was a three days walk - one way.

So, after much preparation Bartholomy and Aloisious were ready for their pilgrimage - walk and pray, walk and pray, until they arrived at Altoetting and then- walk and pray, walk and pray, all the way back home.

Bartholomy was overzealous and a bit more sorry for his misbehavior. He came up with a great idea. As punishment, to make their pilgrimage more severe and their repentance more humble, a hand full of hard, dry peas would be put into each of their leather boots.

They carried a rucksack with some food and blankets, and walked from village to village. The first night, as they were getting ready for bed in a farmers' haystack, Bartholomy could not get his boots off fast enough. His feet were very sore from the dry peas he had put in his boots. He took off his socks and massaged them vigorously. He asked Aloisious "Why don't you take your boots off?" and Aloisious answered "No way. I do not want to chase the mice out of my boots in the morning. For all I know, these mice love to nibble on the leather too and I can't afford to have holes in my boots."

On the second day, these two pilgrims started out again at sunrise and promised to have an early rest. They passed new villages. A farmer delivering grain to the local flourmill offered them a ride, on a horse drawn wagon. But they were tough and refused. The farmer shook his head, saluted them and went on his way.

That night they selected a haystack to sleep on that was near a creek. Bartholomy sat down on a stone, took off his shoes and soaked his feet in the cool water to alleviate some of the pain. Aloisious went straight to the haystack and made himself a bed for the night. When Bartholomy returned to the haystack, Aloisious pretended to be asleep so he did not have to answer questions from Bartholomy.

On the third day, they were walking again by sunrise. Both could feel that they were getting closer to their destination and wearier with each step. Bartholomy became curious and a bit suspicious as to why Aloisious never complained of any pain or discomfort from the dried, hard peas in his boots. Every time Bartholomy inquired "How are your feet?" Aloisious started praying, "Holy Mother of God pray for us sinners" and walked on ahead. Late that afternoon, they finally arrived at the pilgrim chapel. They both lined up right away for their confession and absolution.

That same night, they stayed at a Pilgrim's Inn where they got a plain wooden plank bed, no pillow nor blanket. The innkeeper told them that they should use their own blankets because the cost for a blanket was very high, one kreuzer (a coin which was equivalent to the wage of two days work for a carpenter at the time). Aloisious let Bartholomy have the bunk, while he said that his spot was very smelly and quickly moved down to the other end of the dormitory.

After breakfast, they both went to the chapel at nine o'clock in the morning in order to receive their blessings. After all, this was the high point of their pilgrimage.

Once they received their blessings, they spent some time looking at religious souvenirs like paintings, ceramics, carvings, and medallions. Bartholomy bought himself a new rosary made with beautiful black beads. Aloisious bought himself a picture of a Madonna painted on wood and a shiny medallion of St. Francis de Assisi for one crown (one tenth of one kreuzer). With their souvenirs packed away very carefully, they started their journey back home.

Outside the town of Altoetting, a farmer told them that they could save a lot of walking by taking a short cut across the fields, and heading straight for the hill of St. Conrad. They found the trail in the field as it was well trampled by pilgrims for many years. They had to cross a small creek, which was running high because of rain that had caused the creek to swell.

Bartholomy sat down on a rock and removed his boots, took off his pants and looked for a long stick to support him while fording the creek. Aloisious twiddled and doodled, trying to waste time. Bartholomy lost his patience and told him that he did not have to be so bashful, that only the wild animals would see him in his underwear. Bartholomy watched Aloisious remove his boots. There was green mush on his socks and it looked awful. "Aloisious, what is that?" Aloisious could not escape his embarrassment. The peas had been cooked. "Oh, you cheat! You cheated the Lord and yourself! The Lord will never forgive you for that!"

Finally, they crossed the creek and arrived at the other side. Aloisious washed out his socks and his boots and kept on walking barefoot. His boots and his socks were dangling from his pack-sack to dry.

That night they found shelter in a hay shed. They both settled down and made their beds. Aloisious suggested that whoever had the nicest dream that night should get the remainder of the double smoked Tyrolean ham all to himself. They had shared this ham all along the trip from the start. Bartholomy thought that this was a good idea and they made a deal.

The next morning, they were both awake before sunrise. Aloisious was eager and excited to tell his dream. Because he was so very sure that his was the best, he started talking. He said that in his dream he went to heaven and was surrounded by the most beautiful angels, who fed him chocolate-coated strawberry cake and champagne and they were singing Alleluia all night long.

Bartholomy was so stunned he could not speak for a while. Aloisious demanded, "Well, say something or else I will claim my reward."

"Yeah, yeah Aloisious. Isn't it a coincidence that I had exactly the same dream, that you went to heaven and that you feasted on all that chocolate-coated strawberry cake? I was so hungry down here on earth I figured that you would not want the ham, so I ate it in the middle of the night."

They were both still cozy and warm in their hay beds, when Aloisious looked up at his boots and socks that he had hung up in the rafters. He was so shocked he just yelled "NOOO..." His socks were half chewed up and his right boot had a hole gnawed through the side.

"Well," said Bartholomy, "I am sure the mice could taste the cooked peas. Thank the Lord that they did not chew all of the boots and just leave you the socks."

Finally, they arrived back home. Father Martinus and the village elders who listened to Aloisious and Bartholomy's story over a mug of beer welcomed them. They all laughed and retold the story to all their friends and relatives.

By the time Dad finished telling us the story, he had finished extracting the thorn prickle from his sock and foot, and had his shoes back on. He told us to listen carefully, that there was a faint humming sound. We were leery and did not want to be near any wasp nest, or God forbid, a hornet nest. Dad pointed up a spruce tree and said that the humming noise must be made by bees up there because he could smell the honey, and almost taste it in his mouth. When he said that, we all craved honey too as we had not had any in our house for a very long time.

Here we decided to take the shortest route back home and as we passed Mailman Schusters widows' house, she was working in her vegetables garden beside the road. Dad said hello and when she looked our way, we children also greeted her loudly because her hearing was not so good.

"Oh hello!" she said, "How are you all?"

Dad told her that we were just coming back from the woods with some mushrooms and that we had some for her. "Oh, isn't that so nice of you," she said and went in to the house to fetch a glass bowl. She returned with a big smile on her face and Dad put in some boletus, a handful of cantharellus and a few other mushrooms that filled up her bowl. Mrs. Schuster was so happy and thanked us so very much.

When we got home, Mom was very pleased with our harvest. It didn't take us long to make lunch. We all sat around the table, and cleaned and chopped the mushrooms. When they were done the mushrooms went into the biggest pot we had. Mom melted some lard on the stove then added a cup of flour and browned it. Once the color was right, she added hot water and a bit of salt. When the pot boiled, the mushrooms were added and then simmered for ten minutes. Voila, the Royal Mushroom soup was dished out and served with a slice of dry rye bread. Mmmmm! How delicious it was!

After our mushroom meal, it was time to continue our adventure. Dad told us to make a real good smoke can so Rudi and Hans punched holes in the sides of an old can. They started an inch from the bottom and worked their way up. Then they used some haywire to make a long handle.

To test their smoke can, they put wood shavings into it. Then they added some small chunks of wood and lit it with a match. As it burned, it turned the chunks of wood into embers. To make it smoke, they added some moss on top of the embers. It smoked… a lot!

Hans was in charge of the smoke can. To keep it going, he packed matches, spare wood shavings and some wood chunks to refill it. Anton and Rudi were in charge of packing two buckets, two old pillow covers, the pancake flipper from Mom's kitchen, five meters of sisal rope, and one strong S hook. Dad got out the long ladder, and we set off.

We went up the hill in a single file, across the meadow, through a wood lot on a deer trail, then through the underpass of the autobahn. Actually, we went the long way around hoping that no one would see us. We continued up a very steep incline and through the reforested area, finally arriving back to the tree where we had heard buzzing sounds earlier that day.

Dad lifted the ladder and pushed it against the tree while Anton and Rudi held the bottom down as a counterweight anchors. As the top of the ladder touched the tree a small dry branch snapped off and fell down on the ground near Anton. Dad warned us to be very careful, because there were many more dry branches up there and he didn't want to see any landing on us.

Hans got the smoke can ready. He added a little dusting of dry tree sap and it smoked profusely.

"Perfect," said Dad while he slipped his belt through the bucket handle and secured it to his back. He then put the pancake flipper in his belt near the bucket, and tucked the corner of a pillowcase into his pants. He went quickly and effortlessly up the ladder. He tested the first thick dry branch, and it broke off very easily.

"Dad, be careful!" cried Franz and Dad answered "You bet I am very careful. It is a long way down to the ground!"

Dad tested two more dry branches and they too snapped off easily. The fourth one didn't break off, but Dad did not trust it with his weight. He held on to it, but just enough to keep his balance. By now, a handful of bees were circling around him. Dad swung the smoke can and the bees went away. As the smoke can was working very well Dad secured it to the highest rung of the ladder using his S hook.

He then found an area on the tree that was completely closed off with bees wax. Very gently, he carved a small chunk of honeycomb out of the hive using Mom's pancake flipper and deposited it into the bucket. Carefully, he continued carving out honeycomb until he filled the bucket. Then he covered it with a pillow cover to keep the angry bees away.

When Dad came down the ladder, we were excited about the treasure in the bucket. He was sweating profusely, and this was not good because the scent of human sweat agitates bees even more and who wants to be stung by them? Hans quickly replenished the smoke can while Dad dried his face and forehead with his red-checkered handkerchief. He also fanned himself with the other pillow cover so as to cool of quickly.

We divided a fist size of honeycomb into 5 equal parts and tasted it. We had to chew it a bit to extract the honey from the wax and then we spit out most of the wax. It was absolutely delicious!

Ten minutes later, Dad was ready to climb up the tree again with the second bucket. Again, he secured the smoke can before getting to work. This time he also carved out honeycomb chunks from a little higher up in the tree.

He worked carefully because he did not want to disturb the queen's inner quarters where the young bees were being nursed. He inspected every scoop carefully. When the second bucket was full, Dad came down the ladder. As he dried the sweat off his face, we noticed that Dad had quite a few stings on his neck. He told us that it did not hurt, but we were not so sure about this. Maybe he wished that it did not hurt.

"Let's go home now," said Dad. " We did very well today!"

Anton and Hans carried one bucket, Rudi and I took the other. Franz was allowed to carry the smoke can home, but he had to extinguish the embers first.

Franz protested, "But Dad, there is no water around here." We all laughed. Dad put the long ladder on his shoulder and Franz put out the embers by peeing on them behind the tree. It was time to go home.

At home, we let the honey drip out of the wax combs into a pot. Then we filtered the honey through a screen and put it into glass jars. We warmed the wax only slightly, to extract some more honey out of it. In all, we got five and a half kilos of honey that we stored away in our secret cellar in the floor, under the kitchen table.

Dad made a deal with the beekeeper nicknamed Honey Peter. Peter offered to give us, in exchange for information on the location of the wild bees, an amount of honey that was equal to the weight of the bees and honeycombs that we led him to, plus three extra pounds. This was a great deal for us.

The next weekend, Peter, Dad and us boys went back to the bee tree. They put up the big ladder and Peter went up with his beehive basket. First, he secured the hive basket to a branch higher up. Then he opened the top lid of the hive and inspected it. He carved out a big chunk of honeycomb from the center and, with a quick check, confirmed that he had part of the queen's chamber and put it into his basket.

The bees were getting very agitated and angry because humans were messing with their home. There were a lot of them swirling around Peter. We wondered why he did not use smoke to keep them at bay. Peter carved out another big chunk of honeycomb and put it into his basket. He was thrilled that he had gotten the biggest part of the inner chamber. He closed the lid and came down the ladder.

"If the queen is in the hive basket, by tonight, all the other bees will be in there as well. We just have to leave them alone. We will come back at sunset to collect all of it."

We went back at eight that night. Peter had left his ladder at the tree. He knew no one would take it because his name was carved into it. All the bees had settled in the hive basket and were calm. He climbed up the ladder, closed the entrance and exit slots and then he disconnected the hive basket and came down.]

The daylight was fading. Peter went up the ladder one last time. He took the rest of the beehive. He filled a special container that had a lid and handle and brought it down. Peter carried the beehive, Dad his ladder, Anton and Rudi carried the honey basket and we the youngest boys walked behind and we all went to Peter's place.

We were fascinated with all the beehives and the equipment that he had. Peter balanced the scale and put the beehive basket on it and the honey bucket on top of it. The total weight was twelve pounds. He subtracted the weight of the hive and the bucket, which left a total of three and a half kilos. Peter gave us three glass jars of honey which weighed at least ten pounds! He thanked us and asked us to let him know if we spotted any more wild bees. We thanked him and went home.

By this time the sun had gone down and a light breeze cooled the air. Like a magician, Dad took a foldable linen shopping bag out of his pocket. He used it to carry the honey home so he wouldn't accidentally drop any.

We arrived home all cheerful and very happy. Mom was waiting for us with warm milk that we spiked up with our treasure of the day. Dad had black roasted barley coffee.

Years later, Dad built our own big bee house and Dad became known as the "Honey Toni." Over the years, he collected a lot of our own honey.

CHAPTER 7

DELICIOUS BREAD

Bread was often made in stand-alone bread ovens that were made out of hard brick. All of the large farms in our area had large brick ovens that stood like little houses outside of the main farmhouse. They had double steel doors, and chambers for both building fires and baking.

Oh boy! Did it ever smell good when the baking was in progress. On our way to school, we could smell all the bread baking in the ovens from really far away. In autumn, these bread ovens were also used to dry fruit like apples, pears, plums and even mushrooms.

Many farmers baked their bread once a week, usually on Wednesdays. A few farmers baked theirs once every two weeks. The bread got drier and drier the older it got, but was still edible. The most common types of breads that were made were whole wheat, multigrain, and sourdough rye. These traditional German breads are denser, harder and crustier than common store bought bread. Loaves were made in different shapes and sizes, weighing anywhere from one and a half, to four kilos.

The farm women made the dough in huge wooden troughs. First, they weighed and sifted the different kinds of flour, depending on the recipes. Bread recipes had been handed down for generations. Sifting the flour was very important to fluff it up and to remove any bugs, ants or grubs. As the flour was milled and stored for periods longer than three weeks, it was normal to find tiny black flour bugs in it. Once the sourdough starter, milk, yeast, and salt were added to the flour, the mixing began. The dough was kneaded until all the lumps were out. It was amazing that some of those frail looking women made such wonderful bread, as it was extremely hard work kneading the dough.

When the dough reached the right consistency, it was covered with a damp linen cloth. It was kept warm near the kitchen stove and left to rise overnight. In the early morning, it was kneaded again and divided into individual round or oval loaves. They were left to rise one more time before they were ready for baking.

The bake chamber in the outdoor ovens had to be thoroughly cleaned before being used, as the bread was baked directly on the bricks. Fires were lit in the bottom of the oven, the night before the baking was to start, usually around 10pm, before bed. The fire had to be built and maintained so that by early the next morning the ovens had the perfect temperature for baking. The loaves were placed into the oven on long hickory paddles. The larger loaves were placed in first, at the back of the bake chamber. There was an area in the middle of the oven that was always left empty. The smaller loaves were placed around the center and closer to the oven door.

Bread was a luxury in our house. We did not always have it. Our mom made bread for us, but flour was scarce and hard to get a hold of. She stretched what little flour we had with potatoes, cornmeal, oatmeal or whatever else happened to be available. Unlike the bigger farms, we did not have an outside brick oven. Our mother baked bread in our kitchen oven. We had a cast iron stove that had a roasting box to bake in. It always came out of the oven super delicious. Mom always gave us a little to taste while it was still hot. She really had to guard the bread from us hungry boys! We would have eaten it all right there and then!

Bread baked with oatmeal was always very crusty and lasted a long time in your mouth. A bite needed thirty-two chews before you could swallow it. The hardest bread, was the one Mom made with bran. You almost needed a saw to cut off a slice. The breads made with coarse mashed potatoes and cornmeal were both delicious. My mouth still waters when I remember my Mom taking the bread out of the oven and smelling the wonderful scent of fresh baked bread.

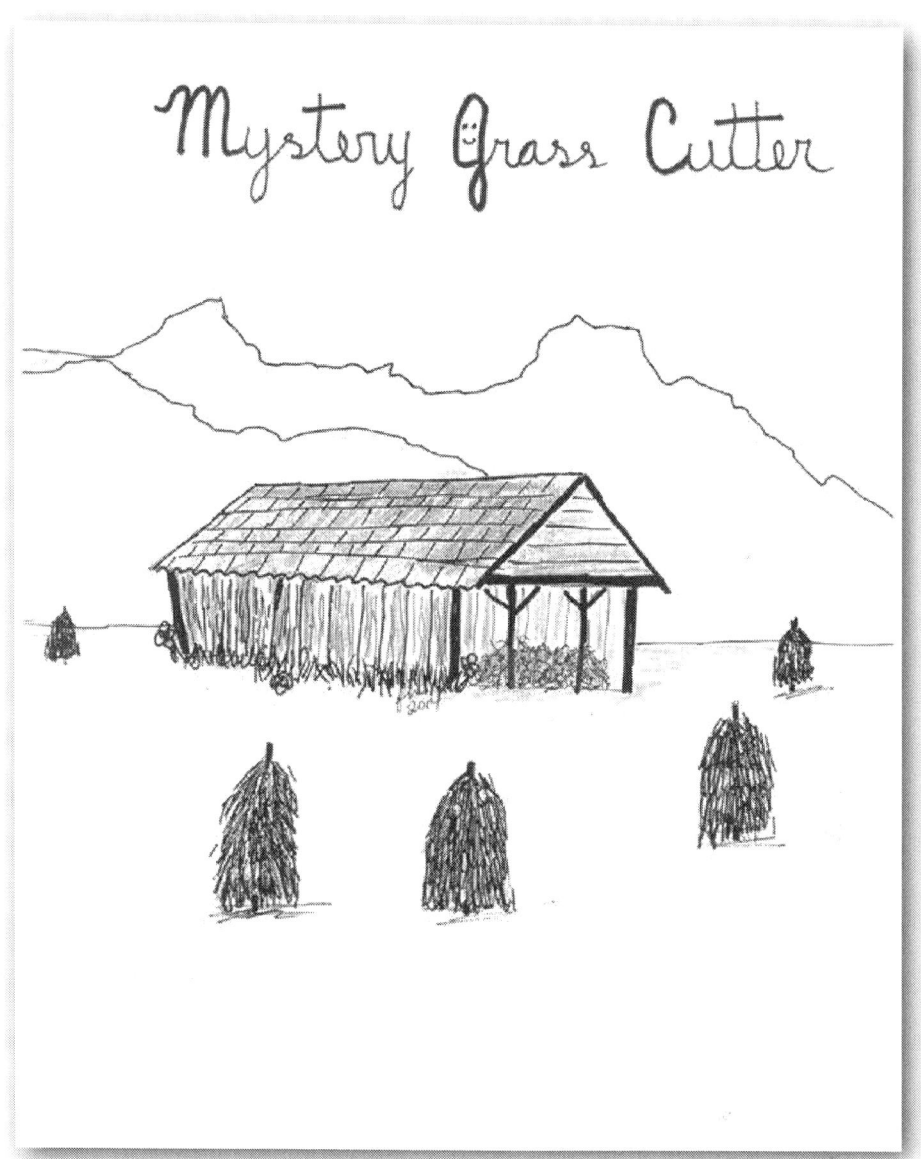

CHAPTER 8

MYSTERY GRASS CUTTER

At the beginning of July 1944, Dad was a soldier and was away at war. We had two goats, one sheep, five hens and a rooster. Mom was alone with us five young boys, and had to take care of it all.

One morning, Mom woke up at sunrise and saw to her surprise, that a large section of our meadow had been cut with a scythe. Very neat rows of wet, tall grass lay on the ground. Now that the hard job of cutting the grass had been mysteriously done, Mom put us all to work harvesting it. We all had to work hard and spread the grass out evenly with hayforks so that the sun could dry it. Since we only had two hayforks, the rest of us used our hands.

The sun warmed the air up very quickly, so by early afternoon, the drying grass was ready to be turned over with wooden rakes. The rakes were hand crafted out of specially selected hickory wood, which made them very sturdy and light. We walked offset from directly behind each other, lifting the hay with the rake at an angle and dropping it again. This action turned the hay over to the wet side up and the dry side down.

It was a terribly hot day, so we children cooled off at the creek. It felt so good to have cold water splashed on us.

Before sundown, we raked the hay into a giant elongated heap so that it could further cure overnight. At the supper table, we all guessed whom it was who had cut the grass for us in the middle of the night. None of us had heard or seen anything, so it was a real mystery for us.

The next day was as sunny and hot. We spread the hay out again for the sun to do its work. In the afternoon, we turned the hay over once more. By five o'clock it was ready to be raked together and loaded onto the wagon. We used a large sturdy hickory ladder wagon that had runners that looked like ladders on all of its sides, to cart the hay to the hayshed where we unloaded it.

We had to make many trips to the hay shed but it was all worth it. At the end of the second day, we were all very proud and happy with what we had accomplished. We reckoned that we had by this time about forty percent of the hay that we would need to feed the animals through the cold winter months. But, we never did find out who did the nice deed of cutting all that grass for us.

Us children loved to play in the hayshed. We would climb up to the rafters and jump down into the soft hay. What fun we had! The children in the neighbourhood also joined in the fun.

For many years after, the mystery of who had cut the grass dominated our supper table conversation. Hans suggested that the "heinzelmannchen" (the fairy dwarfs) had cut the grass and he said that if we had left the grass as it was cut, then the heinzelmannchen would have also turned the grass to make the hay. Hans was very, very sure of this. Anton suggested that it could have been our neighbour Mr. Aicher, but Mom said that Mr. Aicher was too old and frail to do this type of work and would not have been able to do even a small fraction of what was done. Rudi suggested that it could have been the priest, but Mom said, "Old Lenz (the priest) surely does not know how to even handle a scythe, as he has never had to do any hard work in his life!"

Mom suggested that it could have been more than one person and that maybe it was the Hansen girls. Their Dad had perished at the beginning of the war so they took over doing all the hard work on their farm. They were also well known for their good deeds in the neighbourhood, but Mom concluded that if it had been them, they would have cut the grass during the day-time. The sound of the wet stone against more than one scythe would have been heard, especially at night, when all was quiet.

2 Hard Boiled Eggs

and one Slice of Hard

Rye Bread

CHAPTER 9

TWO HARD BOILED EGGS AND A SLICE OF RYE BREAD

Everyday in May, June and July in 1945, refugees, soldiers and war invalids walked by on the gravel road between our neighbors to the North and our house. Some only had packsacks on their backs with bare clothing essentials. Some pushed wooden wheelbarrows with a wooden wheel that had a metal rim, with all their belongings stacked in it, and sometimes even little children were transported in this way. Those who were more fortunate had a small Leiterwagen (a small cart with four wheels). It was rare to see a family coming down the road with horse and cart. In most cases, these people were women, children and elderly grandparents. The single men that came by were usually from captured or disbanded units from the East side of the Oder or the Neisse rivers.

There was one man in particular who greatly impressed me for I was a very young boy. My heart feels heavy every time I think back to this poor man's situation. This man hobbled down the road on his good left leg carrying a crudely made packsack. For his right leg he had a wooden stump from the top of his knee down. This stump was actually a black and white painted autobahn limitation post about 7 cm thick. He also had his hand and lower arm missing on his left side. On the right side he used a crudely made crutch for support.

The jacket he wore was torn and appeared to be part of a uniform. The pants he wore were made of regular black linen. As he needed to take a rest, he sat down on a large bolder beside the road near our property. While sitting, he asked us children for a glass of water. We told him to come to our house. Mom greeted him warmly, offered him a seat at our kitchen nook and invited him for lunch. His name was Erich Hummel from Laupheim.

When he sat down at the kitchen table, he told us that he was very lucky to be alive, as he was helped out of the lazaret (military hospital) about twenty minutes before bombs destroyed the building. The orderly who had helped so many to evacuate, lost his life during that bombing. Mr. Hummel made every effort to walk west in order to get nearer to his home, trying to stay ahead of the Russian troops. Many people were very kind to him and supported him in many ways. He inquired if we knew if some of his friends and acquaintances had passed by. He hoped we would have remembered them by his descriptions and by their many injuries. Unfortunately, we had not seen any of his friends. He also wanted to know the latest news from the radio, how far to the next city, and many more questions.

Mom fried him two eggs and potatoes that he devoured and enjoyed. She also served him a large cup of barley coffee. He hadn't heard from his family for a very long time. Generally, Mr. Hummel seemed to be a happy man, despite his circumstances. He laughed a lot, but when he mentioned that he had no news from his home a tear rolled down his cheek.

While Mom prepared some food for him to take with him, two hard boiled eggs and at thick slice of hard rye bread, he told us that he had slept wherever he could, in railway cars abandoned in the middle of fields because the rails were bombed, or in farmers hay sheds. He told us with a big laugh that some times there was more than one person sleeping in the hay sheds close to the roads. Before he left, Mom put the food she had prepared in his bundle of coat and blanket that he carried on his back. We said good-bye and we wished him good luck and Godspeed, and he wished us the same.

We children walked with him through the gate and accompanied him for several kilometers along his way. As we walked through the fence gate Rudi asked Mr. Hummel if he believed that his guardian angel was protecting him. Mr. Hummel answered, "For sure! And you children, have one too who specially watches over each one of you."

As we went along, he showed us how he could kick a pebble with his wooden leg. Then we started to sing with Mr. Hummel. We sung "The Happy Wanderer

Song" and other songs like "So ein Tag so wunder-schoen wie heute der sollte nie vergehen"and "Auf de rasa grasa'd hasa und im wasser gumpa't fisch."

Some of the songs he sang in a different dialect so we had a hard time understanding some of the words, but we sang along anyway. He had a loud booming tenor's voice and we were sure that people could hear us singing all the way across the valley. We finally said goodbye to him and we walked back home along the railway tracks.

In the summer of 1965, Mr. Hummel visited my parents while he was revisiting the route he had walked in order to get home after the war. He was travelling with his wife Renate and his 14-year-old daughter. His wife was driving the car.

Unfortunately, I was at work so I missed the visit.

The Fox

CHAPTER 10

THE FOX

Early one Sunday morning just as we were about to leave our property to go to church, there was a big commotion behind our Dad's workshop. The rooster screamed and screeched. Chickens were cackling and obviously very upset. We immediately ran back to where our chickens were making such loud noises. To our horror, two chickens lay dead by the creek. They were lying with their heads pointing towards the water. The chickens had had their necks bitten through.

What a huge loss! A third of our egg laying chickens was gone!

It was obvious that the fox had killed the chickens and had them ready to take across the creek to his den when the coast was clear, to feed his young pups. We never actually saw the fox that day, but we knew that there was a fox in the area. He had escaped too quickly. There were a lot of bushes and underbrush nearby for him to hide in. The fox would have taken the chickens back to his den and taught the pups how to pluck the feathers off and tear the meat to be eaten.

Opa grabbed the murdered chickens and took them to the firewood chopping block. He chopped off their heads and then went to the house. He fired up the kitchen stove and boiled a pot of water. He went back to the chopping block where he poured the boiling water over the feathers. This made it a lot easier to pluck. We all plucked the feather off the chickens so it did not take us very long. Once they were both clean, Opa gutted the chickens and prepared them to be roasted.

By noon, we had a "once in a blue moon" feast of two whole chickens. Even the chicken bones were delicious. Only a few were too hard to crunch and munch.

That Sunday we missed the mass at the church, all thanks to the fox!

We never had any more problems with the fox after that. Now, when I think back, I have a suspicion that because Opa was so mad at the fox, he went after it. I recall that the following winter, a red brown fur with a bushy tail was stretched and nailed on a board up in Dad's workshop attic. I am sure it did not get up there by it self! At the time, it was a criminal offense to hunt illegally for fur bearing animals. Only the local hunter had the sole right to hunt in this area. I also remember that, a few years later, my Aunt Amelia had a brand new fox collar on her winter coat, which suspiciously looked like the skin that had been nailed onto a board in Dad's workshop attic. Still today, I wonder if this was the same fox that had killed our chickens… after all don't all red foxes look alike?

The Flourmill

CHAPTER 11

THE FLOURMILL

Our neighbor to the east, about 600 meters up the creek, had a farm with cows and horses. The family also had a timber sawmill, and a flourmill a little further up the creek.

It was fascinating to watch the big waterwheel of the flourmill go round and round. The water wheel turned the axle that went through the wall. Inside the building, a wheel with a thick leather drive belt turned a long transmission axel. The transmission axel had six different sized broad belt wheels.

The first one turned the drive shaft of the big millstone. The second wheel turned the flour sifter that shook all the time. It separated the husks from the flour. At the end of the wooden funnel, there were two sacks attached - a fine woven white linen sack for the flour and a grey burlap sack for the bran.

The third and fourth belts turned the smaller millstones and the flour separator. The fifth and sixth belts worked the sifters. The flour was poured into the hopper box. A wooden hammer knocked gently on the box frame, releasing the flour on to three consecutive screens. The top screen held the third quality flour. It looked gray and a bit coarse. The middle screen held the second quality flour and the bottom screen held best quality flour that cost the most. Our family could never afford to buy this fine flour.

The miller always wore snow-white pants, a white shirt and a white joppe (jacket). On his head he wore a white cap. Often I wondered how he kept his cloths so perfectly clean. The miller's appearance was very important to him because it reflected the pride he had in his craft. His shoes were originally black but all the flour dust on them made his shoes grey.

He was a short stocky man, who sported a small goatee. He constantly kept a watch over all his wheels, belts and moving parts. He didn't talk much, but when he laughed his infectious high-pitched laugh, his whole body shook with delight. When the millstones were groaning, the belt connections clanging, the hoppers shaking and the hammers tapping, it was an extremely noisy place. If you went to see the miller, you had to shout to make yourself heard.

He was also very quick with his hands. I loved to watch him do up and seal the flour sacks. With both his hands he folded the top end of the sack, forming a neat, perfect crown. He held this in his left hand while he then pulled out about 40 cm of sisal string with his other hand, which he then skillfully wrapped around the crown and tied it up well.

When we got home, all we had to do was pull on the longer end of the string and it would release the knot. I watched the miller many times, but I never figured out how he did it. He was just too quick.

There had to be enough water in the sluice race to drive the big waterwheel. The miller had to make sure of this on a daily basis.

For six months of each year, there was less water in the creek, which meant that the miller had to use the smaller millstone. When he used the smaller millstone, he had to work longer hours, from sunrise to sun set to process the same amount of flour as he did with the large millstone.

In the fall, the sluice guard grill had to be cleaned out because it got blocked up with leaves and small branches that floated down the creek.

In winter, the flourmill was a beautiful sight. It was covered with icicles and ice columns that were as thick as a man, and were about four to six meter tall. The icicles hung from the wooden sluice canal. Wherever the water splashed, ice creatures formed.

Now, are you ready for a secret?

The biggest trout were always at the bottom of the waterwheel. Predators, like the grey heron and wild ducks, were scared of this waterwheel.

One Sunday afternoon, when the mill was guaranteed to be still, my brother and I went for a walk. All the folks from the farm were at a wedding in the next town.

My brother saw some nice sized trout swimming in towards the waterwheel to hide. The sluice was closed so the water bypassed the mill, leaving the water level in the lower channel extremely low. Franz was very good at catching trout by hand. He taught me how to feel for a trout in their hiding places. Once you felt the trout, you had to grab it and quickly throw it onto the grass. We lost a couple of nice sized trout because we were too excited or too slow, but we did catch some!

When it was time to go home, we put the trout that we had caught on a stick and wrapped them in Huflattich, a very big, broad leafed plant. Franz said that he did not think that the miller knew that he had such nice trout in his water. We walked home along the creek, hoping that no one would see us. It was illegal to fish without a license, and the fine for being caught was jail time. We got home with three beautiful large trout.

Mom was very pleased with us, as she loved to eat "truite blue."

Firewood

CHAPTER 12

FIREWOOD

Firewood was a very important heat source for every household. Coal was not available and winters were guaranteed to be very cold. Minus 20 degrees Celsius was not unusual.

People were allowed to collect dry branches or dead trees up to ten centimeters in diameter and tree stumps in the ground from trees harvested years before from local woodlands and forests. Lots of energy and ingenuity was required to wrestle these tree stumps successfully out of the ground.

It all depended on the size of the tree stump. There was a huge difference between the stumps of a one hundred year old tree versus one of a sixty year old. The finer the grain, or the closer the year rings were together, the more resin the wood had. Resin gives off a lot more heat. Stumps from hardwood trees such as the oak, beech or maple were very highly valued and considered lucky to find.

The location of the tree stump and the type of soil it was in, determined how hard it was to extract from the ground. The grey blue ceramic or brick clays were soft and easy to dig. Gravel was not too bad, but tedious work. The hardest to dig, was the hardpan dry brown clay, which required a long nosed pick to loosen the soil and roots before digging it. Another consideration was whether the stump was on a slope or in a flat area.

We tackled tree stumps anywhere, but we preferred those on a slope. We developed a system that worked well for us. First we used shovels and picks to expose and sever the main root that led uphill and then continued to expose and sever all the other roots clockwise around the stump. Then we used a three meter round pole as a lever to lift and free the uphill root from the ground. As we dug, little by little, we used the pole to lift the trunk root up. We quickly blocked under the root every time we gained a few centimeters. We continued this process until the roots were free from the soil.

We used an axe and saw to cut off sections and remove them. Lastly, we split the center with a steel wedge and sledgehammer. This was tedious and unpredictable work as the trunks had very twisted grain and did not split straight. Sometimes as many as eight or more wedges had to be driven into the wood before it split. We used a handsaw to sever the last of the attached wood when the axe could not fit into the split slot.

There were a few men in our village that came home from the war with one arm or one leg missing. Despite this, with only their wives, in-laws or children to help them, they were very successful at removing tree stumps for firewood. Evidence of their perseverance was their huge stock of firewood piled up near or behind their homes and under cover.

One of these men was Wiggy Schwarz. He had a solid body and strong muscles in his one arm and legs. He worked steady – not fast – but at the end of the day he had accomplished a lot. Usually, he worked from sunrise and went home by 4 p.m. Wiggy was a happy man who always had a smile on his face. He loved to sing as he went about his work. Wiggy taught us some of his tricks on how to successfully extract some of those difficult tree stumps and we were very grateful for all his advise. He used as much leverage as possible, with his special hickory pole that was five meters in length and fifteen centimeters in diameter.

The kitchen stove was the only heat source in our house, so it was the warmest part of our home. Our bedrooms were upstairs and we had ice flowers on the windowpanes most of the winter. We put clay bricks on the stove and in the roasting chamber to be heated up. When they were hot enough we wrapped them up in a cloth and put them into our beds. First we warmed up where our upper body would be and then we pushed the bricks down to our toes when we got into bed. We were very cozy.

We always left a window open, as fresh air was considered healthy. In the mornings, it was tough to get dressed because our shirts, pants and socks were freezing cold. There was a mad dash to get down to the warm kitchen. Opa was always ready at the kitchen sink to help wash our faces with ice cold water. We hated the ice-cold water in our faces, but we loved and respected Opa so we quietly submitted to his ministration. We dried up using the towels hanging on a clothes rack above the stove. They were warm and cozy. We always kept our shoes in a big drawer under the kitchen stove, so they were nice and warm.

Opa had his bedroom on the northeast side of the house, which was the coldest room in the whole house. He stored two dozen apples carefully on top of his coat cabinet. They lasted all winter because they were frozen solid. Whenever he decided to take two apples down to the kitchen, he would declare a feast and the whole family expected to get a share of it.

Opa certainly took his time and made eating the apples a big event. First, he got a plate ready. He put the two apples on it and placed them on the edge of the kitchen stove by the water container. Next, he took out his stiletto knife (a special pocket knife) with a deer horn handle and sharpened it. It was only eight centimeters long. When we asked him why his knife was so short, he told us that it was originally much longer but it got broken off so he had ground a quarter round tip on it. Then came the time to bring the apples over to the kitchen table. Opa asked the Lord to bless the apples, the food, and all of us. He thanked the Lord that all was well. Finally, he would split the apples in precisely eight pieces. They were still frozen solid and like glass inside. They tasted super sweet. We sure enjoyed them and ate them slowly as we sat together around our kitchen table-nook, by our warm stove, which was burning wood from tree stumps.

The honey
Bees

CHAPTER 13

THE HONEY BEES

On a sunny, hot day in June, we were all sitting at the table enjoying our lunch consisting of cream of wheat with preserved applesauce. All of a sudden, out of the corner of her eye, Mom saw a swarm of bees flying by, just above the vegetable garden. She shouted, "Bees!" and pointed with her hand towards the garden. Quickly, we jumped up and ran out of the house to see what it was that Mom had seen. There was a big swarm of honeybees that was already a hundred meters away and slowly flying East.

My little brother Franz and I grabbed two empty buckets and ran after them. Our bigger brothers collected the water pump, a large wicker basket and a burlap sack from the storage room near Dad's workshop before joining us. After about fifteen minutes of chasing them, which seemed forever, the bees settled on a high branch on a beech tree near the bend in the creek.

My brothers Hans and Rudi went down to the creek to fill the buckets with water and when they were full they carried them to where we were keeping on eye on the bees.

The water pump was something special. It looked like an oversized bicycle pump, with a meter twenty hose attached with a nozzle at the end. This pump was excellent at spraying large distances and hitting its target. The nozzle could be adjusted for a fine spray. It was probably designed for spraying fruit trees with lime water in late fall to keep the ants and bugs away. The pump was put into the bucket and the pumping action instantly started spraying a very fine jet of water that was directed right above the bees.

The bee colony settled down and hung in a clump, which looked like an upside down boot on the branch. When they seemed to be well wetted down and were busy fanning themselves with their wings, Hans and Rudi went to get the big wooden ladder. They attached the wicker basket to the third rung of the ladder, and lifted it up so that the basket was right under the bees.

Rudi climbed up the ladder and gave the branch one sharp hit. The bee colony slid off the branch and smoothly into the basket. He covered them with the burlap sack and came down the ladder. Carefully, we lowered the ladder and took the wicker basket off. A few bees zoomed around but they didn't attack. We carried all the equipment and the prize bees home. We let the bees rest in the basket in the shade while we put away all the equipment.

It was my turn to empty the water pump and there was only a cup of water left in it, so I aimed it at the big boys and sprayed them. They laughed and promised to get even with me later.

"No time to waste" Mom said. "Take those bees over to our neighbor."

The neighbor, Herr Seiler, was a beekeeper and maintained between twelve and fifteen beehives in his bee house. They were very nice people and very religious too. One time, I had to deliver a message and I had to wait outside the door for a very long time because they were praying and saying the Rosary. Then they had their dinner and then they attended to me.

The Herr Seiler was the Official Community Milk Inspector. His job was to go on his bicycle to all owners of cows, sheep and goats, and measure the quantity of their milk and record the result in the Official Milk Production Book. A copy was sent every week to the District Commissioner of Agriculture and there it was determined how much milk the animal owner's were allowed to keep for themselves and how much milk they had to deliver to the Milk Board.

They had a small house with four acres of land that was enough to feed three nanny goats. By gravel road, the Seiler's house was seven minutes walking distance away, so we took the shortcut and crossed the creek and meadow, and arrived in half the time. We gave Herr

Seiler the bees. He thanked us very much, but emphasized that the bees had escaped from his bee house. We left for home a little disappointed because secretly we were hoping for a small reward.

But Mom said, "Those neighbors are quite poor, and they have nothing to give. Everything is just fine. Rewards come in different ways and times. After all, did you not have fun collecting those bees? And on top of it, you boys are now expert bee collectors because none of you got stung!"

The Secret Cellar

CHAPTER 14

THE SECRET CELLAR

We had a Secret Cellar!

Our grandfather, on our Dad's side, had built our house. His name was Anton and he was a master cabinetmaker. He had made all the wooden furniture in the house by hand. There was no dining room in our house, so we ate in the warm kitchen. We sat together cozily on a three sided kitchen-nook bench and table. The built-in nook bench had back panels that were made from very fine-grained larch wood. This wood was rare because it came from very high up on the Tyrolean Mountains from trees that were over a hundred years old and were expensive to buy. At the top of the back panels was a six-centimeter crown molding. There was a window on the middle wall that was decorated with a twisted iron curtain rod and a cheerful curtain. The print on the curtain fabric depicted dancing girls and boys in traditional costumes. Six large cherry wood plates sat on top of the crown, three on either side of the window for decoration. Our kitchen was the heart of our home.

Our Grandfather originally made three of the wooden plates on a very ancient and primitive wood lathe. The other three were a little bit smaller than Grandfather's plates, but our Dad had made them. We had watched him make them on his wood lathe. It was fascinating! To make them, he held the razor sharp chisels against the wood turning on the lathe. Wood chips curled off and fell to the floor. To finish the plates, Dad rubbed them with bee's wax, which gave them a matt shine.

I never knew Grandfather Anton, because he passed away five years before I was born. I loved to listen to stories about him and what he was like. As a hobby, he led a music band on weekends. There were always weddings, festivals and special occasions where he played his violin and other instruments. Music was his passion. His very favorite instrument was his gypsy violin. He loved every minute he played it. Our father inherited it from him.

It was Grandfather Anton who built the secret cellar into the house. To get to it, we had to move away two chairs and the kitchen table. Then we had to roll up and pull out the thick linoleum floor covering. Next, we had to remove the large lid. It was a meter by a meter twenty, and matched the floorboards perfectly. If you did not know precisely where to insert a flat sharp metal object like a knife, you would not find it easily. Once the lid was removed there were stone stairs leading down into the cellar. There were plank shelves installed all around on the concrete walls.

In the summer and fall, Mom preserved fruit in large glass jars. She sealed them with red rubber rings between the glass jar and the glass lid and stored them in the cellar. If times were very good, Mom kept any spare lard in a blue stone crock. She covered it with wax paper and stored it in the cellar. It was always cool down there as it was below ground level.

When the war was declared over, there were many men and women who were homeless and wandered from place to place. Not only were they the local German people whose houses had been bombed, but there were also many homeless foreigners. Many of them were Eastern European POWs who had been captured and brought to Germany to work on farms, sawmills and factories. They could not go back to their country of origin because they were unwittingly considered "traitors" and would face extremely harsh penalties. With their own countries not wanting them back, their futures were uncertain. To survive, some of them stole food and other things at gunpoint. A story circulated that scared us. A family nearby had been reluctant and resisted handing over their food reserve. There was an altercation, and an old man got shot in the shoulder. So for this very reason we kept our cellar top secret!

Later on, a lot of these roaming people were able to immigrate to South America. Argentina, Brazil and

Paraguay were the first countries to welcome people without nationalities after the war. There were four foreign men who lived in our village. They had worked and lived on farms and sawmills. They were polite, hard working and had learned to speak a little German. Mom told us that it was not their fault that they were in these dreadful situations. They missed their families and relatives very much. We were happy for these people when they were eventually accepted into new countries. We said a prayer for them and wished them well in their new lives, as we sat together on our kitchen-nook, above our secret cellar.

The Christmas Tree
1947

CHAPTER 15

THE CHRISTMAS TREE

Awell-known tradition in Bavaria is that every family displays a fresh Christmas tree during the festive season, which runs from December 6th – also known as St. Nikolaus Day – to January 6th, Epiphany.

As we lived out in the countryside, everyone in our family kept a sharp eye out during the year for a perfect symmetrical spruce tree. The nicest ones always grew at the edge of the forest or in an area where the big trees had been logged at least ten years earlier, so the new growth was the right size. You could not buy a Christmas tree where we lived nor could most people in our area afford to buy one, yet every family or household had a beautifully decorated Christmas tree at this time of the year.

Small landowners, with a few hectares of land would never cut a spruce tree from their own property. Instead, they would sneak onto the larger properties or farms to get their tree. Everybody did this! They just had to make sure you didn't get caught, because that was an embarrassment for the family. The big landowners would make sure that word was spread that "so and so" got caught stealing a Christmas tree from their property. They would send the policeman to write out a warning and that alone was very embarrassing because the other folk would say, "He was stupid enough to be caught!"

My older brothers, Rudi who was ten years old and Hans who was eight, had some trees picked out and their locations memorized. They knew exactly where they stood. You had to have more than one tree picked out because chances were great that someone else had an eye on the same tree as you had.

On Sunday December 7, 1947, it was snowing lightly and the snow was knee deep on the ground. We children were on our way home from the church that was about 3 kilometers up the hill, and our home was in the low spot in the valley near the creek. We had our toboggans with us and we linked them together. The snow on the road was hard packed because the farmers had packed it down with their oxen and horses when they dragged timber to the sawmill. Every village possessed a sawmill especially when it was near a creek that supplied the power for their large waterwheels.

The leader or pilot of the toboggan team, usually my oldest brother Tony, would lie down on the first shorter toboggan. He hooked his feet into the front end of the second toboggan. Rudi, my second oldest brother, laid on the second toboggan with his feet hooked into the third toboggan. The rest of us, Hans, Franz, and myself pushed, ran and then jumped onto the third toboggan and away we went. We went, faster and faster, hoping that no oxen or horses were on their way up from the valley. Sometimes we went too fast or it was too icy, but there was no way to slow down. If we had to stop or get off the road, we had to roll over into the deep snow -with lots of laughs and giggles. The road had three sharp curves, and near the end, a double S curve that was always icy. On the east side of the road there was a long and deep ravine that had to be carefully avoided – not that we were scared of it, but it was a very long way to climb back up to the road again.

There were always other toboggan teams trying hard to beat us, but we were just one second ahead, in the lead. The curves came up quickly and the other teams could not pass us on the inside. Some learned the hard way and lost control and ended up down the ravine. Tony was an excellent pilot. He calculated the approach into the curves well. Thus we would arrive home in a very short time.

At lunchtime on this particular day Mom asked us to go find a Christmas tree. We got our sleighs ready to go up to Tafenreuth, which was the home of a single farmer, two kilometers up a steep hill. This hill was the steepest in the whole area, which gave us the fastest run. However it was also a demanding climb. It took us one hour to get to the top. We passed by one of our prospective Christmas trees, which stood at the edge of the forest owned by landowner Emil Schmalz. Sure enough someone had gone to the tree and had shaken off most of the snow, and then had gone back in the same tracks where they had come from. We noticed that whoever left his footprints in the snow must have worn some military riding boots. We concluded that it must have been Emil himself, so we continued on. We went on straight across the meadow to the road, where it was a lot easier to walk, even though it was icy.

Emil's mother Rosalana was the matron of the family. She never smiled and seemed to always be grouchy. Her first husband had died early in their marriage. She remarried her husband's brother Hans. He was a tall, quiet fellow with one gold earring in his left earlobe. The local herbalist, Rybe, had advised Hans to wear a gold earring in the opposite earlobe to his weak eye in order to improve his eyesight. We never did find out if it actually made a difference or not. He was the only man in the whole village that wore one gold earring which made us children eye him suspiciously.

Rosalana was well known for being a very greedy woman. Many people, such as refugees from the east or families who had lost their homes through bombing air raids in the city, were trying to gather food by begging, buying, bartering or trading anything they still had in their possession. Rosalana would ask for their wedding rings, necklaces, earrings or any other jewelry in exchange for a small loaf of bread or a five kilo bag of potatoes, vegetables or fruit that were in season – taking full advantage of their desperate situations. She would give these people the overly ripe vegetables or fruit, while she still had better quality ones in the back of the barn. Our Mom thought that this was disgusting and despicable and she had little regard for Rosalana.

Shortly after the War had ended, Emil came home highly decorated with close combat medals. He was honored and celebrated by the local folk, and he certainly enjoyed all this special attention. Emil also had a high school education, which very few people in this region could boast about. Ninety five percent of the men left school at age fourteen in order to apprentice in a trade. The folk in the village who knew him said, "Aaaaah" and "Ooooh! What a hero he must be!" Only a few of those medals were given to soldiers in all of Bavaria.

Emil was worshiped as a hero until Erwin Schupp, who was one of his military companions, came to visit. They both ended up at the local inn for a few drinks. There the innkeeper's ears got longer and longer while he listened to Erwin's stories… spilling the beans and letting the cat out of the bag.

Erwin told everyone that he and Emil were adjutants at the military supply office depot in Waldeck, a small town near Dresden. Most of the buildings were destroyed by the British Air force in a bombing raid near the end of the war. Their unit was then disbanded.

Erwin and Emil had each grabbed a handful of medals from the office desk drawer before heading for home. They split up. Erwin went west and Emil went southwest.

As soon as there was an opportunity to acquire civilian clothes, Erwin had bought a pair of pants and a jacket from a war widow with the last of his money. Unfortunately, the jacket was too tight and the pants were too short, but the widow was very kind and let the pants out at the cuff and set the buttons of the jacket closer to the edge of the seam so that it would fit him a bit better. Before sunrise, Erwin discarded his uniform with the medals behind a pilgrim chapel. As he continued on his way, in a ditch beside the road he found an old dilapidated bicycle that had definitely seen better days. He learned very quickly that the tires were made of solid rubber, which made the ride rough, but he thought that it was better than walking.

Erwin went on and on, talking about their adventures. Emil regretted the day but the damage had already been done as word had spread fast and wide. Men returning from the war and war widows regarded Emil as a sly louse for lying, and never forgave him. Emil tried hard to overcome the stigma by bragging and talking down to the trades people and pretending that he was smarter and better in every way. I am sure they listened only with one ear because they needed his business. Even I could tell by listening to Emil at the blacksmith shop that he had a problem with his ego.

Mom always told us that such people, who try to walk so high in life, are bound to tumble down at some time.

Around 5 p.m., we were home again but without a tree. We had had a fantastic day zooming down the snow-packed and icy gravel road. Franz always knew when it was time to go home, no matter where he was or what he did. At 5.15 p.m. there was a children's story program on the radio and we listened to it attentively. Franz would not miss the story program for anything in the world. How he knew that it was time to go home for the story program I still don't know. He must have had a built in clock!

We told Mom that by the coming weekend, we would have our Christmas tree.

The rest of the week passed very quickly. The weather remained cold and more snow had fallen. On Sunday December 21, which happened to be the third Advent Sunday, the Usher in church lit the third red candle on the huge Christmas wreath that was suspended from the ceiling by a long cable. The Priest read the story of Mary and Josef's journey to Bethlehem from the bible. While the story was interesting, our minds were partly focusing on the fun we would be having in the snow and bringing home the Christmas tree.

As we left the church, it was custom to dip your index finger into the holy water that was in the copper container recessed in the wall at the door, and make the sign of the cross. The teenage girls of the village were playful and dipped their whole hands into the holy water and sprayed us boys in the face, giggling as they went out.

Excitedly, we tobogganed down the road to the valley. Six other sleigh teams tried to beat us, but we were faster. Once home, we got our skis ready by putting a little red candle wax on the bottom of them. We used Mom's iron to melt the wax evenly on the bottom of the skis. Mom was not pleased at all with us! She was horrified and envisioned red wax stains on Dad's white Sunday shirts and on her white blouses. She made us clean the iron thoroughly while still hot on a damp cloth. Then we had to clean it with fine sand from the creek. We returned the iron to Mom cleaner and shiner than it had ever been before. This iron had been a wedding present from her second cousin, Augustine who lived in Switzerland.

Shortly after lunch, we left for the Renzel Hill. The Renzel family had their farmhouse near the top of the hill. They had a superb, 360-degree view of the whole area. The snow on the hill was pristine and untouched. Opa Renzel, the head of this family, had fallen off the ladder while picking cherries right after he came home from the war. Consequently, he was wheelchair bound for the rest of his life. He was a very upright and well liked man. I was so impressed by him as he always had a kind word for everyone.

Downhill
Tobogganing.

The sky was overcast and more snow was expected. After thirty minutes of trekking, we arrived at the bottom of Renzel hill. To make a perfect ski run, we first had to pack the snow. We all lined up perpendicular to the slope with our skis on, the bigger boys first and the smaller ones below, and began trampling the snow one step at a time. Most of the snow got trampled down by the bigger boys and we smaller ones had it easier following them. We warmed up quickly so we took off our mittens and wooly tuques. Oh that felt so good! It took us a good forty-five minutes to pack down the snow all the way to the top of the slope. Time was going by very fast.

As soon as we arrived at the farmer's hay shed we turned around and finally skied down on our groomed trail. We went back up the hill using big V steps, which went much faster. It was so much fun.

After several runs, Anton and Rudi decided to build a snow ramp to do some ski jumping. They stuck ski poles into the ground then secured them with the other poles. They braced the skis against the poles, which formed a mold for the jump. We all helped gather snow and quickly filled up the mold on the uphill side. As we put the snow in, we trampled it to make sure it was hard and compact. When we were done, the ramp was one meter high and two meters wide. Franz went over to the edge of the forest and broke off two pine branches, about fifty centimeters long. He stuck them on either side of the ramp as markers that we could see from all the way up the hill.

The ski jumping went well and we had very few wipeouts. Rudi held his jump record of nine meters, Hans and Anton were right behind with eight and a half meters, while Franz and I jumped between four and four and a half meters, which was not bad for our age and size. Although my knees were a little bit wobbly (or so it seemed on the way down to the ramp), we did great!

Around 4 p.m. the weather started to get worse. The temperature dropped some more, the wind increased, which in turn whipped bigger and denser snowflakes sideways at us. The visibility was now reduced to only about three meters, so my two older brothers decided to call it quits and went straight home. Hans, Franz and I decided that is was perfect weather to try and get our Christmas tree without getting caught. We skied down to the chapel on our property to retrieve the small handsaw and the ten-meter rope that we had previously stashed there.

The chapel was very small and had only room for twelve people in it. Its altar was dedicated to St. Joseph. This chapel was built around 1900, by Italian emigrants working at the brick factory nearby. However, after twenty years of operation, the factory ran out of high quality clay and closed down. The workers went back to Milano and Torino, but left the chapel behind. Our grandfather on our Dad's side looked after the upkeep and repairs, in memory of those foreign emigrants and their families, and then our parents looked after it. Interestingly the brick factory was demolished and not one single brick was left standing but the little chapel has survived over one hundred years by now.

At the chapel, we stuffed the rope and the saw inside Hans's sweater. We proceeded on, in a roundabout way, to the clearing where our potential Christmas tree was. Thankfully, the silvery spruce tree was still there so no one else had claimed it. While Franz shook the snow off the tree, Hans got the wrapped saw out from under his sweater and handed me the rope. We used our skis to dig the snow away from the base of the tree trunk.

Hans started sawing at the base of the tree but his sawing sounded very loud to us, as everything else was so very quiet. We were trying very hard not to be heard or seen.

Suddenly, we heard the loud crash of dry wood snapping nearby in the forest. Hans stopped cutting and we all listened for more. We imagined Emil standing there watching us. After a few minutes Hans continued sawing the tree. Halfway through the trunk, it was my turn to saw. I knelt in the snow and pushed and pulled the saw against the green wood. Luckily, the saw was very sharp and cut the wood easily. There was another crash much nearer. A dry branch broke off a tall spruce tree and fell, bringing down a lot of snow with it. That is when we realized that Mother Nature was complaining to us as we were stealing her baby tree.

When we finally finished cutting the tree, we pulled it out of the way. Then we went back and evened out the snow in order to cover our tracks. We hoped that the falling snow would make it look like the tree was never there. Luckily, the wind had increased and the snowflakes were falling heavier. And it was also growing dark.

We quickly roped up the tree and then Hans and I pulled while Franz walked behind us. We walked out on to the road that had been recently packed down by the farmers' sleigh teams. For the next fifteen minutes, it was very quiet with not a soul around. Then, we heard faint bells in the distance, on the horses collar, ringing.

We quickly put the tree upright in the snow, at the bottom of the ditch beside the road and we continued trekking on our skis with not a minute to spare.

Hartl, the sawmill owner came down the road at full speed, with his horse and sleigh team, trotting. He passed us at the curve in the road. We waved at him, but he did not reciprocate back. Just as well, we thought. Maybe he had snow in his eyes. He had certainly lots of snow on his cloths and hat.

Soon it was quiet again so we retrieved the tree and continued on our way home. In the dense snowfall, we crossed paths with our neighbor Addie Madina, a big boy who was 13 years old. He carried two small Christmas trees, one for his family and one for the other refugee lady and her two daughters who lived in the same building. We waved at each other and continued on our way.

Some fifteen minutes later we arrived home with our trophy. The whole family came out to inspect the tree. "OOhh…. This one is a really nice tree," our Mom said and Dad agreed with her.

Mom had dinner ready for us and we were very hungry. In the supper prayer Mom thanked the Lord for the special tree and us boys for harvesting it. We stored the tree for the night in the laundry room so that the snow could melt before we decorated it.

After supper the next day, the whole family got involved in setting up and decorating the Christmas tree in the hallway. The tree was secured in a special base, where there was a small pot of water at the center of it to feed the tree. It had four wedges to secure the tree, and four legs so that it could not tip over. Mom directed the whole operation. She told us where to put the tinsel. She emphasized many times, to be careful with the tinsel and the baubles, as they were already nine years old and we would be needing them for a long time to come. We also decorated the tree with candleholders that held half used finger sized red candles that were only to be lit on Christmas Eve. The final touch was the Angel that had to be put on the highest point of the tree. It was always Dad's duty to place it there. The entire family was pleased to see the tree decorated.

The following Tuesday, Emil came to our home to order an oak table from our Dad. As Emil left the house he commented, "Oh what a nice Christmas tree you have." Dad answered, "Thank-you Emil. Ida, my wife, and the children did the decorating."

The highlight of the year was always the celebration of the birth of Christ the Savior on December 24. Everyone dressed in their finest. Mom prepared a special goose dinner. We got the goose from a farmer who needed some work done in his kitchen earlier on in the year. Dad was thinking ahead and ordered the goose to settle his account with the farmer- who was also very pleased. So that year, whenever we walked by Jacob's farmhouse, Dad pointed at a specific young goose and said, "This one is ours and it will be very special at Christmas time."

Franz asked Dad, "How do you know that the black and white one is yours and not any of the other brown and white ones?"

Dad answered, "Trust me boys, I know!" and he left the question open.

Mom roasted the goose crispy and tender, with lots of gravy. She served it with blue cabbage and potato dumplings. Mr. and Mrs. Pikel, and their daughter Nora, who were refugees from Hungary and lived in the largest room in our house, were also invited to eat our festive meal with us and of course they were delighted to do so.

After dinner the celebration heightened. Mom handed out small presents that she had made with love, like mittens, socks, wooly hats and other small handmade knitted items that were very needed. Some other items were bought for very little money and some toys that Dad had made with love. We children thanked Mom and Dad with big hugs and kisses.

Once the presents were opened, Mom played the piano while Dad played the violin. We all joined in and sang Christmas carols until 10.30 p.m. Mom made hot chocolate and served a hand size gingerbread cookie to each one of us. This was heaven - it just could not get any better! (Many years later I was told that Dad had received schnapps for furniture he had made, and he traded the schnapps with the US soldiers who gave him chocolate in return. At the time, this was a risky thing to do and was against military occupation orders.)

By 11 p.m. the whole village was on their way walking to the Church for midnight mass. People were in a cheerful and happy mood. They shook hands and wished one another a Blessed and Merry Christmas. The old priest named Laurence Donner, who had black teeth due to prolonged high fever as an infant, celebrated the Christmas Eve Mass that evening.

The four red candles in the Church were finally all lit on the giant wreath suspended from the ceiling. A fully decorated spruce tree of about two meters high with lots of lit candles stood on the right side of the altar. On the left side, there was a nativity scene. Behind the manger was a hidden candle that was lit. It illuminated the star that reflected light onto the baby Jesus, while the sheppards, sheep and mules were looking on.

All the ladies and young girls occupied the pews on the left side of the church and the men the pews of right side. I wondered who came up with that idea - maybe the Bishop thought that the congregation could concentrate better on praying if they were separated. The organist played 'Silent Night' extra loudly and everyone sang the best they could. It felt as if the sound was shaking the whole church. The priest read the story of Jesus' birth from the bible and then offered communion. The organist played some more hymns and the parishioners sang with all their might. By 12.30 p.m. the midnight mass had ended. As people left the church grounds, they exchanged greetings "Frohe Weihnachten"

(Merry Christmas).

On our way home, we went as fast as we could on our sleighs, down the icy road. This time we invited Mom to sit on the last sleigh of the team. Dad went down the valley with his friends from the music band. They piloted a huge sleigh that could easily take 12 to 15 people. This sleigh was usually used to pull hay down from high up on the mountain to feed the animals. Either a person, a donkey, pulled it or a mule equipped with a special harness. It was very well built with a frame low to the ground and two big curved horns bending backwards up front. Behind each horn was a man sitting who piloted the sleigh. The only way they could steer it was by dragging their feet on the floor, snow or ice, forcing the sleigh to move either left or right. Dad and the musicians were laughing and giggling as they went by. Peter the Cartwright played the trumpet loudly while sitting in the back. What a riot they had.

In later years, when we got a little older, we thought that we could have a similar experience with that big sleigh going down a different hill. However, we lost control, turned over, and ended up with one broken horn. Eventually we had to tell Dad and he was not pleased. But, as no one was injured, Dad was not too angry with us. He managed to rebuild the broken horn and we had to promise never to go on it without him.

We had many rides after that with our Mom and Dad and many friends.

St. Nikolaus

CHAPTER 16

ST. NIKOLAUS

December sixth is a special night in Bavaria. Every year on this night, St. Nikolaus came to our house. His three helpers - the Krampuses, accompanied him. They are similar to the devils, fearsome creatures with deer horns and dark outfits. Some even had skin like a goat. Their faces were black and ugly and they grunted. When they arrived at our house after supper, it was pitch dark outside. They rattled their chains and banged on our shutters with twigs and dry branches. It was very scary and it frightened us children.

We were all sitting on the bench around the kitchen table, when St. Nikolaus finally entered the house and the Krampuses followed in right behind him. St. Nikolaus was dressed with a bishop's cap, a red cape, black pants and black riding boots. His ample white beard seemed to be curly like sheep's wool sheered off a sheep's back. In his left hand he held a long staff that was curled on top. A white sack, which looked like a pillowcase, hung over his right shoulder. In his right hand he carried a very thick old book.

St. Nikolaus leaned his staff against the wall and put the white sack on the kitchen credenza. He opened his old book and searched under "M" where he found our family name, then each of our names. He began reading aloud, in his deep baritone voice. One by one, he read out the naughty things we each had done during the year. Then he read a list of things we needed improvement on. Each time St. Nikolaus finished a sentence, a Krampus would jump foreword and hit us over the head with a branch. It made the Krampus happy to punish us in this way. We were not stupid! We knew what was coming, so we covered our heads quickly with our arms and hands. The Krampuses grunted sternly and rattled their chains excitedly, to show off their powers.

This was a very dramatic event for us children. After the last boy was read his misgivings, St. Nikolaus stepped in closer to the table but his helpers stayed a bit further back. Now he found a list of the good deeds that each one of us had done and he carefully read them out to us – and there were many! I am sure St. Nikolaus forgot a page or two, because there were a lot more good deeds that we had done that he did not mention.

At the end of his speech, St. Nikolaus retrieved the white sack and presented every one of us with a handful of walnuts, an apple and a special gingerbread cookie. The gingerbread cookie was as hard as stone, with glaze on top and a hazel nut in the middle. We all thanked St. Nikolaus and he continued on his way to visit the neighbouring families.

In order to get to the neighbours, St. Nikolaus and the Krampuses had to use the walkway around our house. Anton, Rudi and Hans went quickly and got three rotten potatoes. They went upstairs and waited by the open window for the Krampuses to come around the corner. The moment they were close enough Anton, Rudi and Hans threw the mushy potatoes at them. They hit one Krampus between the antlers and the rest fell in the snow. The Krampuses went wild! We were afraid that they would come back to us, but since they were not sure where the potatoes had come from, eventually they grunted and went on their way.

In the mean time, Mom heated up some milk, stretched with a bit of water, which we enjoyed while munching our gingerbread cookies. As this was a very special treat, we did not gobble the cookies in one shot, but rather nibbled at them slowly, savouring them over a few days.

CHAPTER 17

THE LAUNDRY HELPERS

When we were just tall enough to reach the wooden laundry table, with the help of a forty-centimeter tall bench to stand on, we were allowed to help Mom in the laundry room. Oh what a lot of fun we had!

The laundry room was a simple room with a very smooth finished concrete floor and a drain in the middle of the floor for the water to run off. In one corner stood the big laundry kettle where the water was heated. Beside it stood the laundry-scrubbing table, with a big window right next to it on one side, and a huge oval bathtub made of galvanized sheet metal on the other. There was also a big jar of liquid soap that Opa had made for us from scratch.

The white linen had to be soaked in light soap water overnight, and then gently boiled in the laundry kettle for ten minutes. We had to use the paddle to turn the laundry over because there were always big air bubbles forming and they lifted the laundry above the water surface. We were kept very busy with the paddle pushing the laundry underwater. Piece by piece, the individual items, like shirts, bed sheets and towels, were taken from the kettle and put onto the laundry table. We used the paddle to retrieve them out of the kettle, but we had to be very careful not to get splashed with the boiling items. On the table, we had to scrub the linen with big hard brushes. These brushes were called "wurzel buerste," which means root brush, but they did not seem to be made out of roots. They were very flexible, tough and strong. I still have no idea what kind of root was used to produce this kind of brush.

Mom scrubbed away at one end of the table, while she kept an eye on us and advised us to watch out for our knuckles. We filled the bathtub with fresh water from the tap and rinsed the laundry in it. It took two boys to wring out one item. We simply folded the big items and then each of us twisted it in opposite directions. We managed to get most of the water out and developed muscles at the same time. We placed the items in the laundry basket. This process was repeated until all the laundry was done. Replacing the fresh rinsing water always took the longest. The reason for this was that we had one well up the hill, and shared it with our two neighbors to the north. In order to have enough fresh water for the laundry, we had to fill up extra large pails and barrels during the night when nobody else was using the water.

After the laundry was done, we emptied the kettle and put fresh water in it for our badly needed baths.

In the winter, weather permitting, the laundry got hung outside on the line. It dried to some extent, but also froze stiff. We had to take it off the line gently because the frozen laundry would break easily. Then we hung it above the kitchen stove where it would dry over night quite nicely.

During the summer months, we hung the laundry out on the line or laid it on the grass to dry. However, one end of the laundry line was attached to our swing set so if there was laundry on the line we could not use the swings. Swinging caused the posts to move forth and back and the laundry flopped up and down and occasionally even flew off.

CHAPTER 18

THE CUCKOO

In the month of May, the weather in the hilly regions of Bavaria, the Black Forest and Austria, is warmer. The fruit trees are in full bloom. The meadows are generously sprinkled with wild flowers. The fragrance of all these blossoms fills the air. The honeybees and insects are buzzing around and are busy collecting as much nectar as they can.

The birds are chirping and singing with all their might. This is the time when they are looking for a mate. The most romanticized bird in this region is the Cuckoo, as he is famous in poems and in songs. If you ever have the chance to go out for a hike here at this time of the year, you would enjoy beautiful views and possibly enormous rainbows that stretch from hill to hill in the distances. And, chances are that you might hear the exquisite song of the cuckoo bird. It is a soft, beautiful melody that resounds from the valley and forests. The cuckoos make their beautiful sounds only in the months of May and June. The rest of the year they are quiet. I always wished the Cuckoo bird would keep on singing.

Behind our Dad's workshop, there was a knothole in the plank siding under the roof, making it a perfect spot for a bird's nest. Mr. and Mrs. Red Robin decided to build their nest in that hole, and they laid three eggs. As both Robins were out looking for food, the cuckoo bird went into the Robin's nest, threw two of the green Robins' eggs out of the nest and laid one of her own. The cuckoo's egg was much larger, also green in color but with a dozen black dots on it. She left the egg there and flew away, thus leaving her egg to be hatched and taken care of by the Robins. The cuckoo birds are always very lazy parents, as they leave the upbringing of their young to other birds.

When the eggs hatched about eighteen days later, the young cuckoo was much bigger than the young robin. And, the cuckoo was always very, very hungry. He grew much faster than the little Robin. As time went on the cuckoo demanded more and more food from Mom and Dad Robin, who were soon exhausted from bringing worms and insects to the little birds from sun rise to sunset. Over the next few weeks, the cuckoo chick grew and grew. Soon, the nest was too small for both of them, so the cuckoo pushed the small robin out of the nest. The young cuckoo chick was easily now double the size of the robin's parents.

It started to develop feathers and diligently practiced flapping its wings. A week later, it jumped out of the nest and flew. Mom and Dad Robin must have been very happy to see him take off. They taught the cuckoo how to find insects and worms. As the cuckoo was always hungry, it learnt very quickly how to satisfy its hunger.

Because people were so enchanted with his song, they developed "Cuckoo Clocks," known worldwide. The makers of these clocks are able to produce the identical sound of the cuckoo bird!

The Hedgehog

CHAPTER 19

THE HEDGEHOG

On a sunny Sunday morning, on the way home from church, we boys went on short cuts through the forests, on deer trails and on farm footpaths. At the edge of the freshly ploughed field, we saw a hedgehog sniffing at something in the grass.

It was a beautiful little animal with a snout like a little small piglet. His back was covered with a million eight centimetre long brown silvery grey tipped needles. We dashed towards it, and as we got there, the hedgehog rolled himself up into a ball the size of a soccer ball. We could not see his head nor his feet once he was rolled up.

Hedgehogs do this to defend themselves against predators like foxes or badgers, who would eat the hedgehog with delight. But, as a big ball of sharp needles, the hedgehog becomes too painful of a meal for the delicate noses. When the fox or badger get near enough to sniff the ball, the hedgehog would just jerk a little and prick his enemy's nose with his needles causing them a lot of pain and often this led to an infection. After all, the nose is the most important organ on the predator faces.

The badger though, has figured out how to defeat the hedgehog when he is rolled up. He is known to roll the hedgehog to any nearby shallow water, which forces the hedgehog to open up and swim away. The badger then attacks and eats the hedgehog.

My brother Hans told me that these hedgehogs are very good to have around the house and garden as they catch a lot of mice and all kinds of bugs and grubs. Our garden had a lot of field mice and they had destroyed a lot of our vegetables and plants. So, Hans took off his jacket and we rolled the hedgehog into it. We were very careful not to get pinched by his needles. We took him home, each holding one end of the jacket.

On our way home, we passed a gypsy caravan. They had just arrived at the village square in their self contained brightly painted in red, yellow, green and blue wagons. Their wagons were pulled by their circus ponies. Each wagon had one pony up front and two right behind the first one. They were starting to set up their show tent, merry go round and ability stalls.

We were fascinated to see these gypsies. They were short people with dark eyes, dark complexions, and well-tanned skin. The men wore their long shiny black hair tied up in ponytails. They had lots of children with them.

The gypsy queen was a very pretty lady of about eighteen years of age. She had two very long braids with bright red ribbons at the end. She wore a matching red blouse with frills on the collar and on the sleeves. Her skirt was long and black, with a dark green and bright red wavy trim down to her ankles. She wore soft handmade sandals and had bangles on her ankles and had two huge earrings, which appeared to be made of gold, hanging from her earlobes. Her necklace was made of shiny transparent glittering bird-eye pebbles. They for sure did not come from the area where we lived!

When the gypsy Queen noticed that we had a hedgehog with us, she became very friendly and wanted it badly. First, she offered us free entry to their circus show, but we declined. Then, she upped her offer with extra merry go round rides. We declined again. She told us that they would bake the hedgehog in clay, gypsy-style, and have a feast. That really made us hold on to the hedgehog tighter. Finally, she offered us pony rides, which we really would have liked, but the hedgehog was more important to us. We considered this little hedgehog to be our friend and therefore it was our responsibility to protect it rather than see it be baked in a clay casserole.

Hans signalled me with his eyes to move on. As we started to walk away, the gypsy Queen followed us so we did not go straight home. First, we went up the hill. She followed us at a distance. Maybe she figured she could catch up with us easily, or maybe she hoped the hedgehog would escape from us and she could then catch it. But, as soon as we reached the edge of the forest, we turned sharply and went down a short ravine and into a culvert with little water in it. This was a long culvert that crossed under the autobahn. We came out by our familiar creek, which had plenty of shrubs and bushes on either side of it, and we did not have to worry about being detected.

Unfortunately, we startled the wild ducks that were swimming in the water and they flew away, making a lot of noise. We were worried that the gypsy Queen had spotted us with all the duck noise. But as we hid, we watched her wander away in the opposite direction with a frustrated look on her face.

As soon as we got home, we let the hedgehog go by the empty hay shed. It had a strong wooden floor that kept the hay off the ground. It was dry, for a nice warm nest, and there were a lot of hayseeds.

The following weekend, the gypsy circus put on a grand show. We children hung around observing their so-called skill booths, where one could test their ability and their strength. The booths were wagons parked together and opened up on one side. Spectators were encouraged to see if they could be lucky and win a prize. For a fee of five pfennig, you could try to throw a small leather ball (double the size of a golf ball) through a ring, three meters away. If you did, you would win a prize. The prizes were small painted animals made of clay, wood or silk flowers, and other ornaments. We saw only one fellow win a prize. My brother Hans thought that the ball must have been rigged with a pebble inside and therefore being off center, so that it was difficult to hit the target. He said that maybe by twist throwing the ball, one might hit the target. But, we would have had to practice that with egg shaped stones down by the creek.

It did not take long for the gypsy Queen to recognize us. She asked Hans "Do you still have the hedgehog?" We both answered that it had escaped on us. She somehow did not believe us and with a smile said, "You silly children. That serves you right! You are the ones who lost out badly. But, if you find another hedgehog, you know what to do."

The Sunday afternoon circus show was on. We could not afford to buy tickets, but as we were curious we hung around. The canvas tent filled up slowly. First, the well to do big farmers, with all their children, went into the show tent. Then, the sawmill owners went in with their children, followed by some other large families who lived higher up in the mountains and were known as smugglers. These smugglers knew how to get over to the Austrian side and back without being detected. They seemed to be well to do. With the addition of a few more stragglers, the tent was full.

When the show started, we were busy admiring the ponies and the donkeys. The tent flap was closed and extra lamps were put up on the inside posts. The atmosphere was already very mysterious and we could not resist, so we crawled under the canvas into the tent behind the last row of benches.

It was noisy as the gypsy King with his three older wives (who were each about twenty-five years old) made a racket with drums, bells, horns and a trumpet, which the King himself played. A young boy rode on a pony standing up. The pony ran around and around, in a circle so that he and the pony were leaning inwards.

Then, the big show fellow came in. His hair was gathered up in a long ponytail and his long black whiskered beard curled at the ends. His name was Szakjish. He wore a pair of tight, black pants with bell bottom legs, soft black riding boots with multi coloured leather embroidered flowers on the outside. They looked like they fitted him well and that they were of very good quality.

He wore a bright red, long shirt with very wide sleeves. The sleeves had as much material as the rest of the shirt and were adorned with a million mother of pearl sequences, which sparkled wildly, reflecting the light from the many kerosene lamps. At his waist he wore a wide woven leather belt.

Szakjish stood on two ponies, one foot on each animal. He went around and around, faster and faster, his shirtsleeves were flapping like laundry in the wind. The band got noisier and noisier and the audience got more and more excited. Then, he let go of the reins and flipped over forwards in the air and landed on one of the pony's haunches.

The crowd went wild and the noise became horrendous. He went three more rounds standing on the two ponies' haunches. Finally, he flipped backwards and landed on the sawdust floor. The thrilled audience applauded loudly.

As the ponies were still running, Szakjish jumped back onto the back of one of the ponies, and then he swung himself underneath the pony and came up on the other side. How did he do this and not get trampled to death? He got lots of applause and we found ourselves drawn to the front row with all the other children.

Next came a young girl, just a wee bit older than Hans, dressed in sparkling fairy cloths and elegantly riding a sheep, with no saddle. She just held on to the wool. She made the sheep kneel on its front legs then stand up on its hind legs. And she did not fall off! The sheep was very smart and understood everything. Its name was Nelly. The girl asked, "Nelly, is it cloudy outside?" Nelly answered by moving her head up and down. Then she asked Nelly, "Is it Monday today?" Nelly shook her head from side to side. It was very still in the tent and the tension was very high. Now she asked the sheep, "Is it Tuesday, Friday or Saturday?" Nelly answered each time by shaking her head from side to side. How did Nelly know what day it was, when most of the time I didn't know what day of the week it was?

Finally she asked Nelly, "Is it Sunday today?" And Nelly shook her head vigorously up and down. We were so impressed. I wished I had a smart sheep like that at home. Nelly and her trainer received lots of applause and rousing music from the band.

A dog ran into the ring, possibly a Sheltie, with a big Siamese cat on its back. They ran five rounds without the cat falling off. The last round the cat turned and faced backwards. We all thought she would fall off, but she did not.

Then came a very scary part of the show. They put up a huge black painted wheel with four pegs on it. The black wheel was slightly slanted when the gypsy Queen appeared in a tight fitting yellow blouse, a burgundy coloured mini skirt, and soft leather boots up to her knees. All her outfit was studded with thousands of mother of pearl sequences so she just sparkled like a star.

At the same time, the great rider Szakjish entered and stood about ten feet away from the wheel. He opened a red, thick, heavy leather handbag that was full of knives. He took out a knife and a sheet of stiff paper, and then cut the paper into slices with the knife thus demonstrating how sharp both sides of the knife were.

There was a white outline of a person painted on the wheel. The music stopped and the tent went silent. The gypsy Queen spun the wheel and then Szakjish started to throw his knives. The first knife he threw hit the wheel and landed inside in the person's outline. The crowd booed while he continued to throw more knives at the wheel. The next two completely missed the wheel and landed in the sawdust that was in front and behind the wheel. The crowd booed even louder. Szakjish continued to throw a dozen knives. The knives hit the wheel, but half of them landed inside the person's outline. When he had thrown all his knives, they stopped the wheel and collected them.

The gypsy Queen got onto the wheel and stood on the lower pegs, spread-eagled while holding on to the pegs above her head. An assistant rotated the wheel with all his might. The music started very loudly, with drums, bells and horns while Szakjish got his knives ready. The wheel with the gypsy Queen spun around quite fast and it made me dizzy just looking at her.

The audience was entranced and absolutely quiet. Szakjish threw his first knife and missed. It flew right over the wheel. The second knife landed on the wheel beside her right leg, and the drummer made a short rat-a-tat with his drum. Another knife landed above her left hand. Every time another "clack" sounded as the knife hit the wooden wheel, the audience in unison heaved a huge sigh of relief. Three more knifes landed by her feet. The atmosphere got tenser and tenser. Some ladies in the audience bit their fingernails and others put their hands over their eyes.

Szakjish held up eight more knives above his head. He asked the audience if there was anyone who was a good knife thrower and wanted to try their luck. One man sitting in the back row came forward. He was an older man wearing very strong eyeglasses. We had never seen him before.

Szakjish gave him the eight knifes and told the man that if he missed, he would be tied to the wheel next. If however, he throws them well, he would go home with the prize. Szakjish held up a bag of coins and jingled it.

By this time the wheel was turning very slowly. Szakjish turned the wheel faster and gave the signal to throw the knives. The band started to make a racket and the noise was unbelievable. This man's eyeglasses must have fogged up or he was too exited or nervous because all his eight knifes went over the wheel or beside it and landed in the sawdust. I am sure that the audience was as nervous as I was. The gypsy Queen had exposed herself to such great danger.

Szakjish then stopped the wheel and the music came to a standstill and it became very quiet. The gypsy Queen stepped off the wheel and gathered all the knifes then motioned the old man to come to her. When he was up front she said, "A deal is a deal. Now it is your turn to take the wheel."

The man turned quickly and tried to escape, but Szakjish, who was standing behind him expecting the move, held him and pointed to the wheel. He went meekly and the gypsy Queen tied him to the wheel with four red bandanas and a lot of ceremony. With the one remaining bandana in her hand, she blindfolded Szakjish. As she did this, the music and bells went wild. We were all frozen in disbelief.

The wheel was turned and the man screamed. Szakjish started throwing all his knifes in rapid succession. I am sure every one's heart stopped. The wheel was stopped, the music played as loud as possible. The old man was untied and carefully helped off the wheel. The audience went wild. You couldn't see the painted outline of a person, as there were so many knives. Later, I wondered if the old man with his glasses were really part of the gypsy show.

A young lady came into the ring. She bent backwards and touched the floor with her head. She seemed to have no backbones in her body.

The dog came back in and showed off some more tricks. He jumped through a ring then they lit the ring on fire and he jumped through it. Then he jumped through two burning rings. What a smart dog he was.

The gypsies ended the show with a parrot that spoke in several languages. It said "Guten tag. Servus. Dosvidania. Bon journo. Koesenoem zepa." Wow, what a smart bird!

The show was just great and when we got out of the circus tent, the gypsy Queen spotted us two and asked us how we got in. We just pointed at the big farmer's wife who had a lot of children and we told her that she was our Mom. We were sure she paid for all of us. The gypsy Queen smiled at us and we were off.

On our way home, I told Hans that we should start training our sheep and our goats to count. When we finally got home, we told our Mom of our adventure. She just smiled and asked us to make very sure that all six chickens and the rooster were locked up in the hen-house because whenever the gypsies travel to the next village, some farmers missed a chicken or two. No one can say for sure if they ended up in the fox's den or on the spit over the gypsy fire.

So as long as the gypsies were in town we kept a sharp eye on our chickens and locked them a little earlier in the henhouse. They were easy to count because the rooster always sat on the top runner, three hens on his left and three on his right.

A year later, we had a hedgehog family - Mama, Papa and two little ones. They were so cute and they loved their den. They were safe and secure. One day, Mom mentioned at the dinner table that we didn't have as many field mice in our garden that year. She also mentioned that hedgehogs actually hibernate during the winter.

At this piece of information Hans and I looked at each other and smiled as we certainly knew why there were fewer field mice. We were happy!

The Runaway Horse

CHAPTER 20

THE RUNAWAY HORSE

Hartl was our neighbour to the East. One day, things went crazy while he was busy hitching up his big Clydesdale horses to the heavy timber wagon.

He had the right lead horse in place and went to bring the other horse out from the stable to be hitched up too. While Hartl was in the stable putting the harness on the second Clydesdale, the first horse got spooked somehow and ran away with the heavy wagon behind it. The horse and wagon tore around the farmhouse, down the road and onto the main gravel road at top speed.

The horse ran faster and faster, and everyone that was on the road had to jump out of the way quickly or risk getting run over. One daredevil farmer boy, who, by chance was walking on the road, tried to stop the horse but he nearly got run over instead. He was just that much quicker than the horse, and was able to get out of the way. He got the fright of his life, but he realized that there was something wrong with the horse because it would not stop.

The horse and wagon just flew by on the gravel road near our house leaving a dust cloud behind it. As it went by, it also made a tremendous amount of noise and commotion.

The horse was foaming at the mouth, the reins were flopping backwards, and his mane was straight back like a flag. The horse ran like this for about eight km, and then it stopped all of a sudden. He must of run out of steam! A farmer from the next village hitched his own horse to the wagon and delivered it back to Hartl.

We children were always afraid of those Clydesdales. Rumour had it that the horse went crazy and Hartl had to sell it. However, the horse may have been stung by a hornet or a bunch of wasps, which would have caused the horse to spook in this way. Hornets were about triple the size of a regular wasp, so we were really afraid of them and kept out of their way. If we had the chance, we would kill them and burn their nest out if we found where it was located.

School Playground Cave-in

CHAPTER 21

SCHOOL PLAYGROUND CAVE-IN

Our school was situated 3 kilometers up the hill from our home, in a village called Höhenmoos. Hoöhenmoos was a cluster of farmhouses around the church situated on a sunny knoll overlooking the Inn River valley far to the west. To the south you could see the spectacular panorama of the Alps. A chain of the Bavarian mountains, from east to west, greeted you in the foreground. Behind them loomed the impressive Tyrolean Mountains known as "The Tame and the Wild Kaiser." Their snow and ice covered white tops, reflected the sunshine back to the village.

The knoll where Hoöhenmoos sits has had inhabitants for a very long time. The church, with its onion top dedicated to Saint Peter and St. Paul, dates back to the year 1,200. According to legend, Bonefatious, with his Irish missionaries, brought Christianity to the area and had the church built by the local residents. The view from the bell tower is a fantastic 360°. The scenery of the mountains and the valley below is breathtaking and is a great privilege to experience.

Sebastian, who sat in school beside me, told us that his house was very old. His family believed that it was a fortress a long time ago. The walls, up to the first floor, were over a meter twenty thick and built the roman way, with mortar made with granite, lime and sand. It was still incredibly strong and very hard to chisel. To do any improvements or repair work to their home was always a major headache for the family. The owner of this building in the early days must have been the "Burg Herr." In other words, he owned the fortress, the surrounding land, and the people or serfs on it.

Other fortresses in this area that had survived the years and were still in good order, all had huge towers. Sebastian's house, five hundred years ago or more, must have had a tower too. But, these Burg Herrs were always at war with each other. The weaker ones got attacked by the stronger ones and were plundered time and time again. Because of this, over time all the fortresses developed secret tunnels deep in the ground for people to escape through or counter attack the enemy from behind. These tunnels crisscrossed the small village. Once the fortress was destroyed, the tunnels were no longer needed so they were abandoned. There were also a number of different deep wells dug to supply water for the inhabitants and their animals. Often, the attackers poisoned the wells before they left so the inhabitants had to dig new ones. This added to the undermining of the grounds.

Our school playground was located by the cedar hedge that bordered the teacher's vegetable garden. One day a hole in the ground appeared in our playground, close to the hedge. It was the size of a soccer ball. At first, speculation was that an underground stream had caused it. The teacher warned us not to go near it, as it could have been dangerous. Many people in the village had very imaginative ideas, and a multitude of rumors and speculations started circulating. This made it more exciting for us children. Some people suggested that an ancient burial ground could have been beneath that spot as the hole was near the church's cemetery plot.

The hole got twice as big after it rained. We children were well aware that this was a dangerous spot, but that just made it more thrilling to throw sticks and stones down into it. We listened to see if we could hear the "plop" or any sounds of the object landing. After the second rainfall, the hole became bigger still. Mr. Schlimmer, the teacher, warned all the children again, but even more sternly than he had before, to stay away from the cavity in the ground. He warned us that if ever anyone of us should have fallen down, there would have been no help whatsoever and we would have found a quick death down there. In order to scare us even more, he told us that there was no air deep down there.

When Mr. Schlimmer was not around, we could not resist the lure to see what was down there. One afternoon, we got hold of a can, a candle, a thin long wire and a long rope. We tied the rope to one of our legs and secured the other end to the nearby apple tree about four meters away. We crawled over to the edge of the hole in the ground and feeling secure, we looked down. We could not see a thing, as it was pitch black down there. We lit the candle, and dripped hot wax into the bottom of the can and quickly attached the candle to the center of the can. With the long wire, we very carefully lowered the can down into the hole. We were finally able to see about five meters down, where there was some black timber, rocks and debris covering the bottom. Just then Peter, one of our boys standing on guard, whistled signaling that someone was approaching.

We pulled up the wire can and candle, and untied the rope from the tree as fast as we could. Then we walked away, over to Sebastian's house, just barely before Mr. Schlimmer arrived at the schoolhouse on his bicycle.

Bordering the school playground stood the village fire hall. It was a small, narrow two-story building. It had an outside wooden staircase that lead to the upper floor. On the ground floor there was one room with a large door, where the very important fire engine was kept. It was a one cylinder, diesel driven water pump, with a five-centimeter diameter hose attached to it, mounted on a sturdy hickory wagon with steel rimmed wheels. The nearest farmer, whose horses would pull the wagon, was situated only fifteen meters away. Almost every farmhouse had a pond with stagnant water nearby to use to extinguish a fire if ever needed. The frogs loved these stagnant ponds and they were very plentiful.

Mr. and Mrs. Plotz lived in the suite above the fire hall. They were refugees from Eastern Europe. Mrs. Plotz was an old, scrawny lady of average height, very active and a bit on the nervous side. Mr. Plotz was also quite old, a little bit shorter than his wife, and had a very wrinkled face, almost like a Don Bosco apple in March. He had only a few hairs left above his ears and they were always standing straight up - giving him the appearance of an owl. His twinkling eyes were dark and moved constantly. His flat nose suited his round face well. He was a likeable person and very friendly with us children.

Mr. and Mrs. Plotz seemed to argue a lot. Maybe it was just their loss of hearing that contributed to that perception. One day, they had an argument just as we were on our school break so it caught our attention. Mr. Plotz held their lacquered and very polished "Volksemphaenger" radio, their only valuable possession, out the window while Mrs. Plotz shouted at him for quite a long time. When Mrs. Plotz had had enough of Mr. Plotz's playing games with their precious radio, she finally lost her patience and grabbed her husband's jacket at the back and tried to pull him and her radio in. Unfortunately, it caused the opposite effect and the radio slipped out of her husband's hands and went crashing to the ground below. Mr. Plotz just laughed while his wife shrieked and went quickly down the stairs to see what the damage was.

At this point she realized that all the school children were standing there staring and gaping at her. She started shouting at us that we should get lost and mind our own business! We were all laughing and that made her even madder. She chased after us with a short stick that she managed to grab from the nearby firewood pile, but there was no chance of her ever catching any of us.

Eventually, Mr. Schlimmer organized parents and other volunteers to deal with the cavity in the school playground. Three farmers, each with their oxen and sturdy hickory wagons, twenty adults and some twenty-five boys and girls all equipped with shovels went to the nearest gravel pit, about a kilometer away. There they loaded the wagons with gravel. The farmers then delivered the gravel to the playground where everyone unloaded it into the cavity. The cavity swallowed all the gravel we could throw down. In all, nine wagons of gravel were dumped down the hole. Mr. Schlimmer calculated that the gravel would settle and more of it would be needed in the future, so at the end of the first day, he thanked all the volunteers and asked them all to come back one more time for one more load of gravel to be left near the cavity.

Even though the hole was safely filled in, we continued to speculate as to why the ground had caved in and what had it been used for in the past? We shared these ideas with one another around the table, by the warm stove in our kitchen.

CHAPTER 22

PANDEMONIUM AND RABIES

Dad acquired a young piglet from a farmer that we could raise to feed our family with.

We built the piglet a stable in the barn, next to the sheep, near where the hay shed was attached. We fed it with all sorts of kitchen scraps, like potato peels, bran from the flourmill etc., and the piglet foraged for whatever it could find in the big yard behind the barn. It loved hayseeds from the bottom of the haystack. When the month of October arrived, the piglet was 4 months old. It had grown and had managed to gain a bit of weight because we had fed it acorns that had ripened and had fallen off the trees.

Fattening up the piglet was very important to us. We took the time to find all the oak trees that grew within a few kilometers of our home. We children competed with each other to collect the most acorns to feed the piglet.

Up in the attic of Dad's workshop, we had six sections of the floor boarded off - one section for each of the children and one for Dad. We put the acorns we collected into our own sections to keep score. Naturally, Dad could only come with us to collect acorns on Sundays because he was too busy during the week working in his shop. We had a great advantage over him as we found lots of acorns on the way back from school. We filled our school bag, our pockets and at odd times we took off our knee socks and filled them up too! Other people also collected these nuts so whoever got there first after a strong wind or a storm collected the most.

On Sundays Dad came along on the acorn hunts and the competition was fierce. Dad managed to keep us children excited, making it a game where chances of winning were fairly high for each one of us. It did not take us long to read Dad's mind and realize that he just wanted us to hone our attention and do better all while having lots of fun.

We did not want Dad to collect more than we did but he used all kinds of tricks to steer us away from the cluster pockets. These were small indentations in the ground, where acorns would roll into when they fell off the tree. It was easy picking in these pockets full of acorns.

Dad could recognize where the best spots were and where the most acorns would be long before we got to the tree. It always made a big difference where you chose to pick - the sunny side of the tree (the south or the west) they always had the most acorns on the tree but after a westerly storm, it was the opposite. There were more acorns on the east side of the tree as the wind blew them there.

Sometimes Dad was leading and sometimes one of us boys was leading in the amount of acorns we had in our spot up in the work attic. Some of our neighbors, who also had sheep or piglets in their stable, were not shy to collect the acorns from the trees growing on our property. But, as long as we were there first to collect the acorns, we were not too worried. We could do the same somewhere else. There were no hard feelings and no one claimed a specific oak tree for himself.

Up in Dad's workshop attic our acorn sections were getting full. Dad made a special rake to rake the acorn so that they would cure properly and not go moldy. In the end, Anton and Rudi won the competition by two buckets. The rest of us were very close in the amounts that we had collected. In all, Dad was very pleased with us. He announced, that in his estimation, we had collected over five hundred kilos and this would make the piglet very happy and strong.

On a sunny day in 0ctober, we boys were on our way from one oak tree to another, with buckets and jute sacks when we passed by a big beech tree. It had been struck by lightning some fifteen years earlier. The bark was cinched from top to bottom. The tree continued to grow and the bark closed intermittently all around, but left a cavity inside. This was an excellent spot for squirrels and for birds to make a nest.

Rudi, who was ten years old at the time, could not resist putting his hand down into the opening to feel how deep the hole was. Suddenly he screamed very loudly – a squirrel or a packrat had bitten him. His index finger on his right hand was bleeding, so Rudi took off his shirt and wrapped around his hand. Howling, Rudi and the rest of us ran home right away, with our sacks and buckets of acorn that we had collected.

At home Mom told us to stay calm and that she would take Rudi to the nearest hospital, which was 15 kilometers away in the next big town. Mom had a small Sachs motorcycle where she could pedal as well as use the motor in order to help her drive up a hill. Together, they went to the hospital to get Rudi his first rabies shot. After all, he could have died from rabies! Rudi and Mom came home two hours later. The doctor had told them that without the anti-rabies shot, Rudi would have been in heaven within a few days.

Rest assured that none of us kids would ever put our hands into the cavity of lightning struck tree again. I am not sure if Mom exaggerated, but when I think back now, every once in a while, we boys needed a reminder of the reality of the dangers out there.

CHAPTER 23

SERIOUS EMERGENCY SITUATION

One day, we boys were busy fighting over a toy – a roller scooter that Dad had made for us a long time ago – and while chasing each other with the broom, we accidentally knocked down a tin can from the top of the tall cabinet that stood in the hallway. As the can fell down, it spilled its grey powder and dusted my brother Rudi all over as he ran by.

Mom recognized the tin can as Opa's Rat poison – strychnine - which is a very powerful poison. She shouted, "GET OUT OF THE HOUSE AND DON'T BREATH RUDI!"

Very quickly Mom got a bucket of water from the nearby garden water barrel and poured it all over Rudi, who was now outside on the lawn. This was an awfully dangerous situation as there was a high probability that Rudi could have died from inhaling all this powdered poison.

Mom continued to pour water over Rudi, then he stripped off all his clothes and he got scrubbed from head to toe with soap and warm water from the kitchen stove water container that was always full of warm water.

Once Rudi was dried, he got dressed with dry, clean clothes.

Mom ordered us to stay away from the hallway area and to start a fire under the laundry kettle. We needed to heat up lots of water, so that we could all have a bath, a rinse and put on fresh clothes. Mom wrapped a wet towel around her face and cleaned up the grey powder from the cabinet, the wall and the floor. She changed the water many times to get rid of the poison. Once done washing the area, she scrubbed every centimetre again, this time with more soap and Lysol.

Hans quickly had the fire in the laundry kettle roaring. He used lots of fine kindling, a basket full of pinecones, and tree bark loaded with sap. As we were not allowed to go through the hallway, we boys had no trouble climbing in and out of the laundry room window.

Opa could not have known that we children one day would knock this poison can off the top of the tall cabinet where he had hidden it. We really had no business being near this can, but then children will play.

We knew about rat poison, but we did not know where Opa had hidden it. We knew that it was a very strong and effective poison because we had watched Opa use it. He made some paste with some lard and that grey powder. He put it in the center of a wooden tube, , and placed it near the chicken coop. There, he had secured it with a big, heavy, flat rock.

The rats often came up from the creek and helped themselves to the kitchen scraps that were meant for the chickens. They became bold enough to raid the chicken eggs. When the rats eventually tasted some of Opa's concoction, they perished almost instantly. Once they had tasted the poison they were only able to move a few steps away. Opa was very stern in warning us to stay away from the flat stone and the area around it. He got rid of those ugly rats pretty fast, but a few months later, others that travelled along the creek also came by to sample the chicken scraps and met the same fate as the others.

We children used slingshots and pebbles and the rats as targets. It was very difficult because these animals only came out after sunset, when the light was fading. Hans was the champion. He killed some with his slingshot and Rudi even got one with a stone that he flung from a distance.

The Sheep

CHAPTER 24

THE SHEEP

Once day in September 1946, Opa Sebastian, our Mom's father, obtained very confidential information from Joseph Marai, the rake maker. While purchasing some rakes, he found out that Wastl Weidenschneider, in the Grassau high meadow Alm (farm) had some sheep for sale.

The Marai family worked together and managed their small and meager Alpine farm during the summer months. In the winter, the women and girls of the family took care of the animals in the stables and all the chores, such as cooking, making cheese from the cow's milk etc. as well as tending to their hobbies like knitting, sewing and weaving. The men and boys were busy in their workshop producing very high quality hickory rakes. These rakes were very sought after far and wide. The Marai family gave a lifetime guarantee on them.

The rakes were all hand crafted - sawed, chiseled, filed and drilled. They took pride in selecting and storing the best quality hickory wood. There was a lot of competition in the workshop – to see who had the best craftsmanship and precision. They treated their tools with utmost care, sharpening them on the grinding wheel and honing them to razor sharpness. They never used nails, only tiny wooden dowels.

The distance from our house to the Marai farm and their workshop was a 4-hour brisk walk, steadily uphill. Opa was happy to borrow Mom's bicycle to transport the rakes he purchased and told us that he came all the way downhill in about 45 minutes, but he had had to use the brakes a whole lot.

Because they were at a higher elevation, the Marai farm had high snow accumulations, usually more than two meters high. This allowed children to side step up the barn roof and ski down on their homemade skis. Often, the Marai family was snowbound and could only get out on skis. Therefore, on weekends, the whole Marai family practiced singing and playing their musical instruments. Eventually, they got good enough to have their own band. They were busy playing at weddings and special occasions.

As Opa arrived home with his 2 new rakes strapped to Mom's bicycle he had a big grin on his face. This made us all eager to hear what he had up his sleeve.

It was lunchtime, and as usual, the whole family sat in the kitchen nook. First, Opa said Grace. Then after the Amen, he informed Mom and Dad that he had great news. He spoke softer and made his announcement very special. He told us that he had information about some sheep available for sale, but that it was possible that they were already sold. In 1946 there was a severe shortage of farm animals. Mom, Dad, and Opa had to act quickly. They calculated that it would be one day's hike to get to the high alpine meadow where the Weidenschneider family lived, and a long day to get back, even when taking all the shortcuts available. The Weidenschneider family farm was in the complete opposite direction of the Marai family farm.

Three of us boys were very eager to go with Opa. Franz was too little, and Anton was in school. We all got our packsacks ready. Opa had a big one with some essential extras, like clothing, blankets, a green over-sized oilskin tarp almost like a poncho, hard boiled eggs, double toasted bread, an aluminum army canteen full of water, a small hunk of speck (cured and smoked pork lard), a First Aid bandage with a needle and thread, a strip of linen, and a miniature bottle of high proof medical alcohol.

Rudi was the oldest boy at 9 years of age. He got Dad's Alpine packsack that he had used as a young, single man for his Alpine adventures in the Dolomite Mountains. It had an embroidered edelweiss emblem and the name "Kurzras " stitched on it. Kurzras was a small town in the Dolomite area. Rudi was extremely proud to be able to carry his Dad's packsack. He felt very privileged.

My brother Hans was 7 years of age. He had his school bag that was a converted horsehide tournister (similar to a First World War soldiers packsack). The brown horsehair was still on the outside flap and you could see that it came from a pinto horse.

I was the youngest at 5 years of age. I had a pack-sack made from a linen sack that had once contained flour, and had belonged to Rudi. Mom had sewn this in 1944 where she kept provisions for each child in case we got bombed out and survived and had to flee the area because the enemy would drive us out. This had happened to many refugees from Eastern Germany. It fitted me well and was not too heavy for me to carry. It just looked bulky because of the blanket that I carried in it.

We were very excited and were looking forward to this adventure. Our parents told us that we would have to go to bed very early that evening because Opa wanted to leave the house by 7 a.m., at the very latest. The next morning we got up at 6 a.m. We ate toasted bread and jam, and drank barley coffee that had been freshly roasted on the kitchen stove with some milk added to it.

The weather promised to be good – in the 20 degree Celsius range – and only a few puffy lamb's wool clouds were in the sky above the mountains. The weather can sometimes change very quickly from sunshine, to rain and wind, and back to sunshine with some more wind, to unexpected hailstorms. All this could happen very quickly.

Dad and Opa discussed the best way to get to our destination using the shortcuts over gravel and farm roads, footpaths, cow trails and even some deer trails across alpine terrain and meadows.

At 7 o'clock on the dot Opa pulled out his pocket watch and let its chime ring seven times. This was the signal for us to hug Mom and Dad and say goodbye. We started off walking straight south, going steadily uphill and through the forest. We came out on the other side where we followed a small trail with a ditch beside it. The water in that ditch was running fast downhill, draining the swampy area above it. The farmers made use of the swamp grass growing there. It was all cut up and stood in many bundles each about a meter and eighty centimeters high. These bundles were known as "strohmandl" (straw men). In this way the bundles would dry and then the straw was used as bedding for the animals in the stables.

On this part of the trail, we could hear a faint sound of ding, dong, dang for a long time. Of course we wanted to know what was making this noise for we could not see any animals with bells around their necks and we heard the sound at regular intervals.

Opa was the first to discover where the noise came from. Someone had built a perfect water wheel in the ditch. It had three cogs, two on one side and one on the opposite side. Three wooden hammers were activated and lifted by their respective cogs on the wheel.

Each cog lifted a hammer up and then let it fall, one on an old frying pan, the second one on an old rusty cooking pot with a hole on one side and the third hammer banged on a plain thin lid. We were very fascinated with this waterwheel and thought that whoever made it must have had a lot of fun doing so. Opa told us that if we listened very carefully you could hear the first three notes of a melody.

The trail turned and it went steeper uphill. Our target was the beech wood hill. It was a knoll surrounded by farmland and its center was covered in beech trees. Only this was very unusual for this area as beech trees were usually mixed in with all kinds of other trees. It was a famous sight to see from far and wide especially in the fall when the leaves turned first to yellow then to bright red. Even on our way to and from school in the fall, we could see the colorful beech wood knoll. It was quite the sight from as far away as ten kilometers. Opa explained to us that it was probably the squirrels that were the architects of this landscape because squirrels absolutely love beechnuts, and therefore they hoard, bury and hide them. And so, unsuspectingly, they plant a whole forest of them year after year!

We continued following the trail as it continued uphill along a narrow valley by a tiny creek. Then we crossed the creek and got onto the next trail, that lead us through a forested area. After a short while we arrived on the south side of that forest patch and came to a blackened building. We children had never seen such a strange looking building before. It had a heavy slate roof and no windows. The walls were brick or stone and mortar, and there were only three walls. The fourth side had a huge barn door on the east side that stood partly open. We looked inside – the walls and rafters were black and on one side there was some sort of an open chimney. Opa told us that this building was used to cure flax, hemp and linen fibers. It had to be soaked first and then broken and lastly dried. The fibers extracted were combed, woven and spun into cloth. Near the building was an empty pond where he suspected that, at one time, held water for the soaking of the fibers. Opa explained to us that in his youth everyone wore linen clothes. But, over the years, cotton was more available, cheaper, and a whole lot softer to wear!

The trail continued up on a steady incline that led us to a mature conifer forest. The trees had unusual coarse bark. Opa told us that the Baron Haklett, who was the landowner in 1860, had bought millions of Douglas fir seeds from his friend Lord Carvan in B.C., Canada. They had planted all those seeds at that time, and they now were impressively tall and healthy trees, much taller than any other local fir trees. We children pried a small piece of bark off one of the trees. It was very porous and light. We stored this in our packsacks as souvenirs and pretended that it was similar to cork but of course it was not!

The trail continued through the forest and we ended up at the elk gate – a three-meter high coarse fence that went straight from east to west as far as the eye could see. Opa opened this gate that had been closed and secured with a simple chain on the post, so that anyone travelling through could open it and close it again. This was meant to keep the elk inside the gate. Now that we were inside the elk gate and on the Baron's property we were hoping to see some elk. These huge animals only existed in the higher elevations.

In the distance we saw the elk's winter feeding trough, with a large shingle roof and triangular hay containers underneath it. Naturally, it was all empty and bare. The ground had been well trampled by the many elk that frequented this feeding center in the wintertime.

At this time some clouds moved in. The temperature dropped and the breeze intensified rapidly. Within a short time a few raindrops splattered down in the distance. "Looks like the weather is changing after all," said Opa.

We watched the rain as it came closer and closer. We ran for shelter under the roof of the elk's feeding trough. We just made it and then it really rained hard. We took our oilskins out of the packsacks in a hurry, as we did not know how long this rainstorm was going to last and we did not want to get wet. It got windier and the raindrops became a lot bigger. Standing under the roof, we were protected and kept dry. Thunder and lightning was at first a distance away. We estimated the distance between the lightning flashes and the thunder claps by counting the seconds - 22, 23, 24, 25… Each second was a kilometer away, so four seconds meant that the storm was four kilometers from us.

The winds and the clouds came over the mountains directly from the East and headed for the big Inn River Valley. After about half and hour, the lightning strikes and the thunderclaps were all around us. We were not scared, as this kind of thunder and lightening storms were common in our area. And luckily, we had the perfect rest stop. We took advantage of the time and ate lunch while we waited for the storm to pass. Hardboiled eggs, toasted bread and an apple provided us with renewed energy. An hour later, the sky cleared up so we packed away our raingear and continued our walk along a small creek. The water had suddenly risen about thirty centimeters and had become muddier.

We came to a fallen tree trunk that we used as a bridge to cross the creek. It had probably washed down the creek quite some time ago. The tree trunk had no branches or bark left on it. It was wet and slippery from all the rain. We crossed to the other side with the help of a long dry stick that helped us keep our balance. As we were walking barefoot, it was easier for us to keep foot control during the crossing. Meanwhile, Opa left his shoes on so he had a hard time keeping upright and not falling into the water.

The trail became steeper and led us around a huge rock formation. It was easily about a hundred meters high and over two hundred meters wide. Small stones loosened up in the higher area and rained down, so we passed the lower area very quickly. Then we went up between this huge rock formation and another higher one. The trail now became extremely steep. With each step we gained about thirty centimeters in altitude.

When we arrived at the top of the rock stone outcrop, we could hear the rushing of water close by, but could not see anything. Opa said to us, "It sure sounds like a waterfall is up ahead somewhere!" Sure enough, around the next rock formation bend there was a beautiful waterfall about thirty meters high and four meters wide.

Our trail went behind that waterfall and came out on the other side, zigzagging uphill. We were all excited to go behind the waterfall, but we did not want to put on our oilskins. Opa went first. He walked behind and through it, and came out on the other side still dry. We were next. There was more than a meter of free room between the water and the rock so we leaned against the rock wall and watched the water falling. It was beautiful! The light reflected from the sun travelled upwards in little spurts, while the water actually ran downward. These reflecting lights were in the colors of the rainbows. We wanted to stay longer, but Opa told us that we did not have a lot of spare time. The waterfall created a fine mist around us that made us feel pleasantly cool.

Back on the zigzag trail, we could see a small mountain hut in the distance. It was above the tree line and looked neat, made with white stones and stucco, timber and a slate roof. It was called "The First Kasa." There were others in the area, but quite far away. As you climbed uphill in different directions, each Kasa had another number – The first was the lowest one, second Kasa was higher up and the third Kasa was even higher up and so on. Opa told us that the word Kasa meant House in the ancient Roman language.

When we got to the Kasa, we looked through the window. It had a fireplace, a large table and rough benches and against the wall there was a row of bunk beds made of planks only. This was a shelter for people who go on hiking excursions in the Alps. People brought their own blankets and sometimes a log of firewood with them whether they need it or not. This way there is always some firewood in case of urgent need for a warm shelter. It also had a crude log bench out at the front.

From here on we did not have far to reach the crest of the Giant Mountain. Once we reached the crest we all sat down on the edge and looked back into the valley and far down where we had come from. We tried to see if we could recognize our home. It was fantastic to see how little the churches were and how little everything else was from this height. Faintly, we could hear the bells of some cows in the lower valleys to the north.

Amazingly the sound of the church bells from the different parishes were easily distinguished from each other, so we concluded that sound does travel upwards.

After a short break, we continued on our way south, finally heading gently down into the next valley. As we walked we could see the Tyrolean Kaiser Mountains topped by some soft white clouds. Opa told us that our destination was in the next valley, just over the ridge. We could see that it was not too far away - to the southeast. He estimated that it would take us another 2 hours to get to our destination.

We took another rest on a boulder beside the trail before heading down another zigzag steep trail. We could see the same trail continuing uphill on the other side of the gorge. Half way down the hill on the other side of the gorge, there was a cable contraption where a man was busy loading limestone on a platform. Once he had a load of limestone ready, he sat on it, and released the brake. The man in his contraption began to very slowly glide along the cable. It gained speed as it went downhill. His momentum carried him along the cable and up to our side of the gorge, to the same height as he had started from.

The man locked the cargo and the cable, then jumped off and secured the load and the platform to the anchor rod. It looked like a steel rail secured in a rock. He carefully unloaded the limestone neatly beside the ramp. He had already amassed a huge pile, ready to be taken down into the valley. The limestone was going to be heated in a special kiln. The end product was white lime to mix mortar with and white wash for barns and houses.

When we got down to the cable, the man was just arriving on our side of the gorge. He was a tall skinny man by the name of Luigi. We all greeted him at the same time. He offered us a ride across the gorge. Opa was a little hesitant but Luigi emphasized that the rock load was three times as heavy as all of us. The platform was certified for a two-ton load, but Luigi never loaded more than one ton at a time. We were definitely not a ton in weight! We inspected the contraption. It had four wheels and two cables, some security hooks so that the wheels could not fall out of the cables and the cables could not fall out of the wheels. Heavy steel rods were holding the platforms and the two centimeter steel rod held the cargo on the platform.

We were really excited to be able to ride this contraption to the other side of the gorge. Opa sat on one end and Luigi on the other, and we boys sat in the middle with our feet dangling down into space. We held on to the safety bar for dear life. Opa held onto the steel frame where the wheels were over his head. Once Luigi was ready he released the brake and the wheels started to roll slowly. We gained speed and in no time we were going so fast we were almost flying. We had no time to be scared and we screamed for joy, while the valley dropped away below us. The noise created by the four wheels rattling along above us on the cables was extremely loud – and it got louder and even louder. We slowed down gradually when we went slightly uphill and arrived on the other side. Luigi pulled the brake, locked the wheels to the cable then jumped off and secured the platform to the anchor rod. We all got off and thanked Luigi for the ride of our lives.

We walked further uphill going in an easterly direction. By the position of the sun in the sky, Opa calculated that it was about 4 p.m. We continued on our trail through the meadow where Wastl Weidenschneider's Alm was located. At this point, we were getting impatient, as we could not see the Alm hut from where we were but Opa pointed at and said, "After the third ridge with the flattened peak - that is where we should be in a short while."

High up in the sky, a hawk was circling. The ground hogs were whistling and announcing our arrival. As we got closer to them, they disappeared quickly into their burrows in the earth. These animals were large and Opa guessed that they might weigh five to seven kilos each. We children wondered if they would make a good meal and Opa confirmed that because these animals only ate grass, they would probably be very delicious if roasted slowly.

This high meadow was full of huge boulders that were the size of a house and some were even larger. These were left behind from the ice age and may have come from the higher mountains to the south. We climbed one of the smaller boulders just for fun and to see our final destination. Opa told us that we had to wait until we passed the next ravine and ridge before we would see anything and that it would be another half an hour before we got there.

Opa realized that we were getting quite tired so he invited us to sing with him. We sang "The Happy Wanderer" and many different songs. This made the time go by faster.

We ran the last two hundred meters of the final ridge. There we sat down and looked downwards at the Weidenschneider Alpine hut, a very old and typical building for this region. It had a foundation of well-fitted rocks. The main part of the structure was made of rough cut wooden beams and planks. The roof was made of slate and had a hayshed that stood nearby. It faced south, and had an elevated patio with a wooden bench and table on it. There were farm animals grazing all over the rolling meadow. Most wore a bell around their neck.

As we went downhill, we were all happy that we had finally arrived. Wastl was just tinkering with his water supply. The water from a small trench went through a wooden gutter, into a big trough made out of a log, out the other end and back into the trench. Wastl greeted us with a big smile. As he lifted his hat off his head and gave us a curtsy he said, "Griass eich alle!"

He was an elderly man of a similar age as Opa. He was thinner and taller, and sported a fancy mustache. Opa introduced himself and us boys and we all shook hands with him. Then Opa explained to him where we had come from and our reason for the visit - to buy three sheep, if possible. Wastl chuckled and said, "Wow! You sure had a long walk to get here!"

He told us that the sheep were just a short walk away, behind the Alm house, up on the slope. He looked up in the direction where they were grazing. "Just wait a minute. I'll call them," he said and then he did.

He made a ring with both his hands over his mouth and it produced a sound like a joddler's, "Ya riee diee dooolioooo." He made that sound a few times. We could not believe that the lead sheep lifted her head up, looked down at us and started walking slowly towards us, with her brass bell clinging and clanging. The rest of the sheep lifted their heads up and looked and then followed their leader.

Opa and Wastl had a general conversation while we listened and waited. It did not take long for the herd of sheep to arrive. They all went directly to the water trough, had their drink and then Wastl gave them each their reward. He had a sack of hayseeds and each sheep got a handful from him as well as a pat on their heads. While the rest of them were patiently waiting around, you could see that they really loved this treat as they happily munched away.

Wastl told Opa to select the three sheep. He helped Opa decide which were the best sheep for milk production. The first one that Opa selected had a black head and the rest of the coat was white. She was already expecting a lamb. The second one was all white. The third one had black spots between her eyes and ears and the rest of her body was white. They all wore their beautiful fleece coat and looked very healthy. Opa marked their ear tips with a thick blue crayon on one side of their velvety ears.

Opa then finalized the deal with a handshake and handed over a hundred and twenty Reich Marks. This was a fortune to have to pay, but Opa paid it out of his own money, as a present to his daughter's family. He also told Wastl that we were planning to leave very early the next morning as we were going to take the longer and easier route back home. Wastl made the comment that downhill all the way would be a lot easier on all of us, including the three sheep.

Wastl invited us to have supper with him. Opa accepted and we children were happy about this. We sat down on the wooden bench by the table in the kitchen nook. Wastl went to the back of his Alm hut and brought out a large jug of milk from the cold cellar storage area. He proceeded to fill the gray enamel coated metal mugs with enough milk for everyone. He then went to the other corner of the room and started a fire in his "Wamsler" cast iron stove. He put some flour into a bowl, added some milk and cracked many eggs into it and with 2 forks whipped it up quickly. He then took a large black frying pan off the wall, added some fat and put it on the stove to melt. While this was happening, he reloaded the stove with lots of small kindling wood that crackled and heated up quickly. Once the fat melted he poured in some of the batter and let it cook. The aroma was heavenly!

While it was cooking Wastl pointed to the stove and said, "Well, it takes time to cook you know!" and he started to whistle a tune "Chopaidi, chopaida." We boys replied together, "Schnapps is good for cholera," at which he laughed heartily. However, Opa, who was very straight-laced, appeared a little embarrassed that his "holy" grandchildren could spill out such language from their mouths. But Wastl's laugh was so infectious that Opa eventually joined in.

The huge pancake took shape. It was nicely golden brown on both sides when Wastl got to work. He chopped it and turned it, added some more fat, and chopped it and turned it some more. He made a Kaiser schmarn! The cooking odor filled the cabin and made us all really hungry. He lifted the frying pan off the stove and put it right on the huge plank table where we sat. A clunky wooden spoon was used to transfer the schmarn on to the ex-military aluminum plates already set on the table. Wastl sat down with us with a big smile on his face. He told us to go ahead and eat well, as he needed the frying pan for the second round. He had lots of batter left in the bowl and there was lots of heat in the stove.

He put a jar of honey on the table. He noticed that we boys only took about half a teaspoon of honey each to put on the schmarn on our plates. We had been taught to use honey very sparingly in order to make it last longer. Wastl told us that he was leaving at the end of the month, and he would not carry the honey back down the valley. He would therefore have to give it back to the bees, and as we knew, the wasps would eat most of it because they are by nature honey thieves. That sure encouraged us to be more generous with our helpings of honey. That schmarn and honey was out of this world, it was so delicious!

Wastl went back to the stove and added some more wood and promptly cooked the remaining schmarn. He told us that since we had come from such a long way we had better fill our hollow legs or we would not be able to hang onto the sheep on the way down. We all laughed at his comment and we thought what a jolly nice man he was.

When the second round of Kaiser schmarn was ready, we were quite full. But Wastl would not hear of it, and emptied the frying pan onto our plates. After all the plates were scrapped clean, we collected them, put them into an enamel bucket. We filled it with some very hot water from the stove and added a thimbleful of liquid lye soap. After it was all washed and put away behind the stove, we were asked to bring in some fresh water to refill the copper reservoir in the stove. We gladly obliged and brought in three full pails of water from the trough.

By this time we were really tired, but Wastl enjoyed our company so he took a zither off the wall and played some local ballads for us. Some of them we knew and we sang along, and some had very funny lyrics that made us all laugh. Opa was right into it and asked Wastl several times if he knew this or that song. If Wastl wasn't sure, he would ask Opa to give him the first few notes of the melody and then he would pick it up. We wanted at this point for the music to go on forever, but finally Opa suggested that we get ready for sleep. We thanked Wastl profusely for the delicious dinner and musical treat. In the hayshed we made nests. We had to put our oilskin ponchos first down, then blankets under and over ourselves, and off we went to sleep.

At sunrise we were up. It was a cool morning. The peaceful clinging of the cowbells so high up in the Alpine region had a relaxing effect on all of us. We washed our faces in the water trough and then let it air dry. We repacked our packsacks and were ready to move on.

The sheep were nearby. Opa took three ropes that were each three meters long out of his packsack and tied them loosely around each sheep's neck. Rudi got to lead the first sheep. Hans was happy to lead the second sheep, and Opa gave me the last rope with the third sheep. We all thanked Wastl again for his hospitality and for selling of the sheep to us.

The sheep walked very meekly, occasionally nibbling on some grass as we walked along. Our trip home was going to be mostly downhill. The terrain dropped very gently until we came to a rock formation, where the trail turned sharply and then became quite steep. The next valley opened up and we had an exceptional view of the biggest lake in the area - the Chiemsee, with the King's castle on an island not far from shore. There were also a bunch of minor lakes to the left, and we could even see part of the Inn River. We stopped for a few minutes and enjoyed the clear sky and the beautiful view.

When we continued our walk, Opa suggested that it was time to baptize the animals. He asked us for suggestions, but we could only come up with boy's names. He was not too impressed with us. He made a few suggestions: To Rudi's sheep he suggested Cleopatra and of course we all loved that name. Hans's sheep he suggested Valencia and that sounded very good to us as well. For my sheep he thought that Mariposa would be a good name.

After the short stop to baptize our sheep we continued on the trail that ended up in a meadow that had rock walls to the south and small hills towards the east and north. This meadow was famous for its herbs. Opa got all excited and told us to start collecting some herbs. We could see lots of arnica, coltsfoot, sage, wild mint, lamb's ears and a few other that Opa pointed out to us as being very good herbs to have at hand. Opa had a handful of old silk scarves in his packsack that he lay out on the ground and we added piles of herbs to each scarf. It did not take us very long to collect a good amount. Opa bundled them up by the stems, and folded the scarves around the herbs. He secured one bundle on each of our packsacks, and all the rest on his.

On our way again we came to a point in the trail where it forked out in many different directions. The first easterly trail led to the village of Freidorf. The west trail went towards to Steinbach and further on to Wangen. To the south it lead to the Giant Mountain up the steep trail where we had been on the previous day. The trail going due north would take us down to the Achen valley, where we wanted to eventually end up.

We went down another ravine trail that led us directly to a hut where a lady was busy hanging out some laundry on a string between two poles. The rest of her laundry was lying on the grass to be bleached by the sun.

There were some animals grazing on the slopes for the summer months. The lady had two braids wrapped around her head and worn like a crown. She wore a long skirt and heavy shoes that suited her very well. After we greeted her, she inquired who we were and where we were going. Obviously, not too many people came this way during the summer. She told us that her family had a farmhouse near the Chiemsee area and that it was her turn this year to look after the animals up in the alpine meadows.

As we walked near the hayshed roof overhang, we saw an impressive looking kettengrad by the firewood pile. It was like a large motorbike, but had a rubber chain link instead of wheels to propel it forward. None of us had ever seen such a vehicle before, including Opa.

In 1945, a disbanded German army unit had abandoned it where it still stood. It still had the army colors. Only the swastika had been painted over. It had a steering handle up front like on any motorbike. Opa estimated that it could probably carry a weight of four hundred kilos or more and that was an awfully heavy load. Opa asked the lady if they ever used this unit. "Well, not really, as there is no gasoline available and if we could get some on the black market, it would be way to expensive to run."

Opa jokingly told the lady that this grand machine could certainly get us all home in less that an hour if it worked! Meanwhile the sheep happily grazed on the nearby grass.

Now the trail led us to a forested area that had dwarf larch and pine trees. As we walked deeper into the woods, the trees became taller and more plentiful. Down the steep slope, the forest environment became more mixed with coniferous trees and some beech and oak. To get through the brush, we had to remove the rope of Hans's and my sheep, so that they could follow the lead sheep easier.

We came to a clearing where the woodcutters had cut hundreds of trees during the last winter, leaving only the huge tree stumps.

Opa suggested that this would be a great place to have a rest and eat our breakfasts, while the sheep graze on the new grass shoots growing nearby. We opened our packsacks and took out our hardboiled eggs and the double baked bread. Opa sliced some of his speck paper thin, to put on our bread. My, did that taste good and we washed it all down with a few gulps of water from his army canteen.

Opa asked us, "How old do you think these trees were before they were cut down?" We quickly started counting rings on tree stumps. Rudi and Hans were pretty good at counting but I was not as able to count like they did. I heard Rudi counting 67, 68, 69 and he had another fifteen centimeters of wood to count, so I calculated that maybe this tree was about 90 years old. I blurted to Opa loudly "Ninety years!"

Rudi and Hans were laughing and said "Ha! Ha! Wait a minute, that can't be right as we are at only at 83, 84, 85."

They continued counting "88, 89, ...91, 92." Opa said that my guess was a very good guess, but that is was best to count correctly. I tried to argue that my brothers might have counted the bark as well, and thereby wiggled out of the argument.

As we got up to continue, we saw a darker spot down the slope in the shade of tall trees. The trail led us down to the spot that turned out to be a woodcutter's shed. As we got nearer, we inspected the crude crafts-manship of the shelter. They had built an A-frame made of young fifteen-centimeter pines poles. The tree bark from the large logs had been immaculately peeled off in single pieces and secured to the pine poles, against each other. They had repeated this process and came up with a double layer of bark on this shelter.

The floor was filled to a depth of thirty centimeters with fir boughs. The one we inspected still had its cast iron stove in it, resting on a big rock slab. Obviously, the workers stayed there all week and only went home on Saturday night, and returned for work early Monday morning.

Further on down, we arrived at another beautiful clearing. It had a meadow on a steep slope where there were at least a dozen cows grazing. These animals trampled down the soil and grass on the slope as they zigzagged their way uphill grazing the grass, in such a way that it made the meadow look like it had steps.

A farmhouse stood at the bottom of the slope and beyond it you could see more forest. The trail zigzagged to the farmhouse and beyond. Opa suspected that the farmhouse was over three hundred years old because the foundation was made the Roman way; the rocks were tightly fitted with sand and burned limestone that got very hard. Plus the walls were thick, over a meter thick. The roof still had grey slate on it.

When we arrived, Martin Weinberger was sitting under the balcony that was heavily laden with bright red geraniums that overflowed down the veranda. He was busy hammering out the sharp edge of his scythe. He was singing as he worked.

He stopped and greeted us and we greeted him in return. Opa told Martin about where we were and where we were going. We refilled our water canteen from the water fountain in front of the house. He invited us to sit down on the bench for a short break so we did.

Frau Weinberger came out of the front entrance a short while later, with a big jug of holunderbeere juice (elderberry juice) refreshments for all of us. Opa and Herr and Frau Weinberger were each given their own cup, but she only had one cup for us boys, so we shared it, and kept refilling it. She was a very talkative lady. She told us that she knew where we lived and that she knew our Dad the cabinetmaker who also plays music.

Opa inquired if they had any news of Jacob recently. They told him that the last time they had heard from him was in 1944 when he was stationed with the army in Russia. They had no idea whatever happened to him.

Opa also inquired how they were doing health-wise, and they replied that besides rheumatism, all was well. He suggested that they should drink more herbal teas and at the same time, he pointed to his bundle of herbs on his packsack behind him. Opa said that some of the herbs would help to alleviate most of the pain. Frau Weinberger complemented him for doing so well collecting herbs – especially since he had such great helpers. We all smiled, thanked and saluted them and continued on the trail.

As the trail was now flat, Opa told us a story about Martin Weinberger's son Jacob and his stroke of luck in a very unfortunate situation. We loved stories, so we listened carefully as we walked.

Jacob was 14 years of age in 1916, when his father Martin had come home from the war in France, for a ten-day leave. He arrived in his uniform, carrying his gun, tournister and helmet. Jacob was intrigued by his Dad's appearance. On his second day home, Jacob watched his father clean his gun and then put it away in the painted cabinet by the entrance to the farmhouse.

A couple days later, while Martin was busy taking the horse to the blacksmith for re-shoeing, Jacob decided to take this opportunity to practice cleaning his father's gun. He successfully removed the breach, cleaned the barrel, and looked through the barrel to see how shinny it was. Satisfied, he put it all back together, but did not realize that the breach pin was still extended on the lock and that the magazine was not empty. So, when Jacob pulled the trigger, the gun went off! There was a huge explosion in the small kitchen! The bullet went right through the ceiling. His two sisters and mother, who were upstairs in the sewing room, screamed. Jacob ran up the stairs, but all three women continued to scream in shock.

The bullet had ripped through the floorboards and had taken some splinters with it. It had travelled right between his two sisters, Kathy and Rosa, within twenty centimeters from either girl! After traversing the second floor ceiling, the bullet ended up in the attic, stuck in the king log of the roof support timber. They all huddled together and thanked the Lord that nothing serious had happened.

When Martin came home, he emptied the remainder of the gun's magazine and hid the bullets. He made Jacob swear never to touch the gun again. After that, the whole family went down on their knees to thank the Lord and all the Saints, especially the angel guarding Kathy and Rosa.

Opa told us that Jacob's bad decision served as a lesson to all young boys in the region who were told his story.

Opa's story surely shortened our trip, and before long we arrived at a place called "Rubeneck". Its name had been inherited from medieval times. As we walked through, it was very quiet. There was no one around as they were all out working.

Opa told us that, within the last fifty years, the word went out that the well water beside the trail had special healing properties. Sure enough, we soon came to a natural spring with water just pouring out of the ground. It had a granite enclosure, two meters in diameter and about thirty centimeters above the ground. The water overflowed and went down into the ditch. Naturally, we all tasted it and we all agreed that it was cool and fresh. But, we could not taste the difference between this healing water and any other water. We even led the sheep to drink some of it.

As we went on Opa told us the rest of the story. The Rubeneck farmer had an aunt by the name of Berta, living with him. They claimed that she lived only on this water and nothing else. People presumed that the well water must therefore be very special. They came from far and wide to fill their bottles to take the water home with them. The farmer did not charge them for the use of the water. However, there was a little sign by the well, suggesting that donations could be put in the mailbox by the entrance to the house. Some people complied generously and others did not. Opa said, "Well, it all adds up."

In 1934, the Gestapo looked into this healing water and they interviewed Aunt Berta. She confirmed that she had only ever drunk water from this well, but she also ate like any other person. No one ever proved that she had claimed otherwise.

The Nazis put up an official signpost beside the well, with their official bureaucratic stamp. It stated that the water was normal, with only the usual local lime and mineral content. The plaque still stood nearby. However, the wording had faded over time.

"So you see," Opa said, "People were expecting that the water was special. The rumors multiplied and this exaggerated their expectations. In other words, they fooled themselves. The only one who came out laughing, was the farmer who emptied out his mailbox regularly over many years."

So happily we continued along the way. The well-behaved sheep impressed us. They now found lots of fresh grass beside the trail to munch on.

A farmer, with two oxen pulling a wagon, filled with gravel, came towards us. We greeted him and he asked us where we had gotten these nice sheep. So we told him up in the Weidenschneider Alm. "Oh," he answered, "that is really far away." He waved goodbye and kept on going. We did the same and moved on.

The sun got really hot and we were due for a rest and something to eat. We happened upon a perfect spot beside the road. A huge hickory tree stood beside the trail and someone had put a bench underneath it. The bench was simply built with two large rocks on either side and some heavy wooden planks on top. A perfect spot for a little rest! We let the sheep graze and unpacked some more of our edibles, although there was not much left. The half hour rest did us good.

So on we went again, on the easy, straight and flat trail. In the distance, we could see the tower of the Steinbach church and the red roofs of houses nearby.

Shortly after we came to a roadside marker with a painting of some raiders on ponies, with curved swords, cutting down a man who was trying to escape. "Yes, this was Simon Schmid, on September 16, 1704" Opa told us, while pointing at the man trying to escape. Simon was the church caretaker at the time, noticed that a strange group of horsemen had invaded the community of Steinbach. While they were busy plundering, killing, raping the local women and burning down their houses, Simon went undetected into the church. He barricaded the heavy oak entrance door, and rang the small bell vigorously, in an attempt to warn the locals that something was dramatically amiss in their community.

Some of the attackers went quickly to the church, but the oak door was locked and barred. While the horsemen were busy trying to break down the church door, Simon barred the bell tower door. He quickly ran up the tower, ripped off his sweater and wrapped it around the bell ringer to silence it. Then, he threw the bell rope down the north side of the tower, opposite to the church entrance. He ripped off his shirt and wound it around his hand, grabbed the bell rope and quickly let himself down.

He then ran for his life for more than a kilometer to very spot of the roadside marker. Here the attackers caught up with him and murdered him. Simon had made it possible for some of the villagers to prepare themselves for the oncoming attack. They were able to defend themselves by loading some of their few guns and chased the attackers away. Unfortunately Simon was murdered a few meters away from a very densely forested area where he would have had a good chance to escape his murderers. All together, we said a prayer for Simon's soul.

From here on, we walked downhill – half was steep and half was flat. We walked straight along narrow cross-country trails, beside fields of grain and potatoes, until we finally made it home around 6 p.m. We were greeted with huge hugs from Mom and Dad and our brothers. They admired Cleopatra, Valencia and Mariposa. They certainly were all eager to hear about our adventures!

The Stray Dog

CHAPTER 25

THE STRAY DOG

In the middle of March of 1946, the bright sunshine reflected from the richly snow covered mountaintops. Some snow still decorated the landscape on the shady, north side of the lower hills, on the edge of forests where the warmth of the sunrays could not reach. On the slopes facing south, very large patches of snowdrop flowers were out and coming into full bloom. It was a pleasant pre-spring day and the air was filled with bird-songs. A million starlings were arriving from their migration and were displaying acrobatic performances "en masse."

A cute, black and white, lean, medium sized female sheep dog appeared from nowhere and was sniffing around the entrance to Dad's workshop. She was excited and it showed in her lively eyes and waggling tail. Dad saw her first and thought that she belonged to a customer coming to collect some finished furniture. But, as time went by, he realized that the dog was there on her own accord. Dad was not worried, as he believed that the dog's owner would show up and claim her, sooner or later.

We kids liked the dog, but we were cautious because she could have been sick or had rabies. Mom had warned us many times to be careful with strange acting domestic and wild animals. The dog seemed to be lost and hungry. We gave her some bread soaked in goat's milk and she gulped it down in one shot. Then, we threw a stick for her to retrieve and she loved that. She retrieved it quickly and dropped it at our feet.

"This dog is trained," said my older brother and we played with her some more. By nightfall, no one had claimed her, so we gave her a little more to eat including the kitchen scraps. She was content and slept in Dad's workshop amongst the soft wood shavings. Some of the shavings clung to her fur and tail and we children thought that this was hilarious.

The following day, no one recognized the dog. We even asked the mailman and the chimney sweeper who came by. As the days passed, we called her Lumpi and wanted to adopt her, but Dad said that we could not keep her. He said that Lumpi needed to live on a farm where she would be useful, loved and fed plenty.

About nine days later, farmer Christian Baumsteiger arrived at Dad's workshop. He was a very relaxed man and always spoke very softly and slowly. He was smoking his very long stemmed tobacco pipe, which he loved to smoke. Christian was walking beside his oxen and his heavy-duty hickory wagon, with wheels that had wooden spokes on iron rims. He always walked with the oxen, ahead of the cart, and directed them where to go. His oxen were large, well fed, and well trained.

On this particular day, Christian came with a load of dry hemlock, maple and beech planks that had been stored for years under the overhang attic roof on the south side of his farmhouse. He was bringing all this wood to Dad so that he would make new kitchen and dinning room furniture for Christian's two hundred and fifty year old farm house.

After all the planks were unloaded and stowed away, Christian and Dad relaxed and chatted for about half an hour. In the meantime, Lumpi was nowhere to be seen. When Christian was ready to leave, he climbed onto the wagon's bench, facing forward, held on to the reins, and gave the oxen his signal call "wiiiihhaaa!" He turned the oxen and wagon around, and then rolled the wagon slowly out of our property and onto the main gravel road. That's when we noticed that Lumpi was following meekly, tied on a leash to the last rung of the cart. She was diagonally opposite to Christian's forward looking seat. He could not see the dog, even if he should turn around.

We asked Dad how he had managed to tie the dog up to the cart so quickly and without Christian noticing. Dad told us that is had been very easy. As soon as he had seen Christian coming, he had known what he had to do. He tied Lumpi up and kept her inside the storage room. The moment Christian sat on the wagon, after he had said goodbye to us, Dad had swiftly retrieved Lumpi from the storage room and tied her to the cart.

A month later, Dad delivered the furniture he had made to Christian's farmhouse. Lumpi was running around and the children, Kathy and Christian Jr., loved her. Christian's wife, Katrina Baumsteiger, was also delighted with the dog. Christian told Dad that after delivering the lumber to our place, picking up some flour at the mill and making some inquiries at the timber mill, he noticed that when he got home, the dog was tied to his wagon. Christian was surprised to find the dog and could not figure out who had tied the dog to the wagon. He had never seen the dog before.

Dad asked Christian if the dog was vicious or if it would bite. Christian replied that he did not think so. Dad held out his hand to let Lumpi sniff it. Lumpi rubbed the side of his snout on Dad's hand and licked it. Dad asked Christian if he wanted to get rid of the dog. When the Katarina overheard the conversation, while she was hanging up the laundry on the line to dry, she said, "No way! We are not going to give up that dog. And, if you Tony (meaning my Dad) want a dog, you will have to get your own. Definitely not this one."

CHAPTER 26

LOTS OF BRICKS

Times were tough. The war was over, but most major cities and towns were partly destroyed by bombs and fire. Opa had lost his house in the city of Munich. He was lucky that he had been in the bomb shelter deep under ground when his house was bombed. Only one wall was left standing, the rest was rubble. Five of his neighbors' houses were hit in the same bombing raid. The destruction had taken only fifteen minutes.

Nineteen people and seven children lost their lives because they thought that their cellars were safe enough to take shelter in. They could not have known that on this bombing raid, the allies were dropping their biggest bombs to date. They dropped the newest, five hundred pound, heavy bombs. They rained down from a height of two thousand meters plus. These bombs smashed through roofs and floors, and exploded in the cellars, effectively flattening whole buildings and causing major devastation.

Brick walls that were left standing were insecure and dangerous. Some elderly men, much older than Opa, risked their lives to tear down freestanding walls with long ropes so that falling bricks would hurt no one. With his home destroyed, Opa came to live with us in our house in the country. We were delighted to have him with us because he was so much fun.

Some people found work as farm helpers and they were expected to work from sunrise to sunset. These people were the lucky ones because they got to eat at the farm. Others had to take any jobs they could get. There were many educated people like university professors, lawyers, doctors, scientists, etc. who were unemployed and who had to do any odd jobs, just to survive. One of those jobs was brick cleaning. Clay bricks were retrieved from bombed out buildings usually by handcart. There had been so much destruction; brick removal was a large part of the clean up.

Our family had piles of these bricks delivered to our home. We cleaned them, and Dad reused them to build an addition to his workshop. We children worked in teams, and got to be very efficient at cleaning bricks. We used special pointy hammers to knock the mortar off and then polished them with a wire brush. It was less dusty when the bricks were wet and the mortar came off a little easier if they had been previously frozen. Sometimes, we cleaned fifty bricks in one hour and nobody could beat that record. Remember there are six sides to every brick. Gloves? What are gloves? It would have been great to have a pair of gloves for this job but none were available. The lime in the mortar was very corrosive and hard on our hands.

At the end of the day we boys were very proud of our accomplishment when another sizeable stack of clean bricks was finished. Mom and Dad praised us generously for our hard work.

Malt Extract Barter

CHAPTER 27

MALT EXTRACT BARTER

On a cold winter's night in 1947, Dad came home with a ten-litre clay pot full of malt extract. That malt extract looked almost like honey. It was sweet and had a bit of a roasted cereal taste to it. We were very happy to have this in our house! Sparingly, we put it on crepes, potato pancakes (reibertatschi), or on plain bread. It lasted a long time, till well after Easter.

Dad had made a deal with a man named Jakob Schwarts, who ran a small guesthouse in a tiny mountain village some 18 kilometres southwest from our home. Some guests had had a disagreement in his guesthouse and had started a fight, which ended with four broken chairs. As a result of this fight Jakob now needed new chairs, but wanted to barter for them instead of paying with currency.

He was a shifty man and kingpin in the smuggler's circles. You could get almost anything from him by way of the black market, but very overpriced of course! Due to the proximity of the border, items were brought into Germany via Austria, carried over the mountains by foot or by skis in the winter. Yes, there were border guards, but the moonless nights, foggy weather, rain and snow storms, were advantageous for the smugglers.

The guesthouse stood on a high knoll with a most beautiful view and was about 1 kilometre away from the village center. The place was decorated in a traditional Bavarian style making it a very sought after place to visit. Most of the clients came from far away, mostly from the city of Munich, because the local people could not afford to pay his outrageous prices. His main business was smuggling good quality coffee and high quality schnapps. U.S.A. military personnel were also his clients. At times, his parking lot was full of olive green coloured jeeps, decorated with a white five-point star on each hood. Jakob also served delicious pastries to accompany his best quality coffee.

Jakob employed a pretty, twenty-two year old waitress named Lisa. She was very friendly with her clients. She collected information for her brother as to who was on duty at the border, when and where. This information was crucial to the whole smuggler's network. There were also some pretty girls up in the mountain huts that kept some of the patrol officers entertained, while Lisa's relatives smuggled goods right under their noses.

If by chance you noticed a border guard sitting in Jakob's guesthouse, you could bet that he was on Jacob's good will list. Border guards who did not accept bribes, were outfoxed and circled around, by taking a more difficult route across the border.

Dad had to make four sturdy solid beech wood chairs with curved back support. It took Dad one week to make these chairs and Jakob paid him with ten litre of malt extract. Because food was so over priced it was an excellent trade for Dad. By today's comparison of value, the malt extract would be worth approximately $230 a litre, which meant that he sold each chair for about $525!

Thanks to Dad and Mom's hard work, we children really enjoyed this small delicious luxury of malt extract.

CHAPTER 28

SEP'S TRUCK

Kurz Sepp lived in the next village, south from where we lived. It was an hour's walk up hill towards the Hochris Mountain to get there. He was one of the first truck owners that operated regularly between his home and the city of Munich in 1947.

As there was no gasoline or diesel available at that time, Sepp powered his truck by burning wood. He had a wood gasifier on the back of his driver's cabin, bolted onto the flat deck of the truck. This contraption looked like a heavy-duty steel cylinder. It had a diameter of fifty-five centimeters and was about a meter eighty high. The lid on the top could be opened and closed with one simple action lever. Through a series of steps in the gasifier, wood was burned to form the combustible gases carbon monoxide, hydrogen, and methane. Theses gases were then piped to the truck's combustion engine and used as fuel.

We watched Sepp put buckets of small cut hard wood into the cylinder, to feed the small fire inside. At the bottom there was a small hole with a metal flap plate on the inside that controlled the draw created by the engine, letting in small amounts of air into the fire-box. This flapper valve was always ringing and it caught our attention. Through the air intake hole, you could see the hot embers glowing.

On the deck of Sepp's truck there was a canvas cover where the rear portion could be opened and secured when under way. There were wooden benches mounted to accommodate passengers, and a big crate with two cubic meters of wood that was secured near the rear gate.

It took about two and a half hours to complete the eighty-kilometer trip to Munich. Sepp departed at five in the morning, at the latest, and he would not wait for any one. People learned quickly to be on time. The truck made an average of 30 kilometers per hour. On the way to Munich there was a long climb up the Irschenberg Mountain, a long incline of about seven hundred meters in altitude and about five kilometers in length. Sepp had to stop the truck and refill the gasifier every hour or so. The stink from that gas was horrendous and one could get sick easily.

There were always passengers sitting in the back of the truck beside the cargo, with the rear canvas flap open for fresh air. In the winter, you had to dress very warmly and take extra blankets to stay warm.

Many times we had the pleasure of travelling to Munich with Mom on Sepp's truck. She was born there and knew her way around. When we were in Munich, we visited our uncles and aunts and were always happy to see our cousins.

On one visit to Munich, Mom dressed us in our finest clothes and took us to a photograph studio. She had previously traded three, nice sized, live roosters for some heavy flannel material on the black market. Then Mom found a tailor who made five jackets, all in the same style, one for each of us boys.

At the photo studio, the photographer had a large tripod with the camera box on top. He lined us up for the photograph to be taken and told us to keep very still. Then he went behind the camera, placed the black cloth that was attached to the camera box over his head, while he held a mercury flash bulb that pointed to the ceiling on a long handle with his right hand.

He shouted, "FERTIG!" and then the bulb exploded! A cloud of smoke rose to the ceiling. He repeated this process again. For me, it seemed to take forever, as I was in a real hurry to go to the bathroom.

The result was that Mom had a great photograph of her boys.

The Huge Elk

CHAPTER 29

THE HUGE ELK

On February 2, 1949, it was cold outside. The temperature was at about -15°Celsius and a about forty centimeters of snow covered the countryside. Early that morning, a huge twelve-tipped horn crowned elk came onto our property.

The whole family was busy enjoying their breakfast in the kitchen nook. Mom and Dad praised all the chores that we boys had accomplished the previous day and told us about the new chores set out for that day, such as cleaning bricks, splitting firewood, feeding the goats and sheep, removing Dad's stack of lumber and piling it up at a better location where it would not be so affected by the weather, etc. There was a lot to do and this would certainly keep us all out of mischief!

When Dad got up to get some more barley coffee from the woodstove, he saw something moving outside in the yard. He looked more carefully and recognized the object walking slowly along in our back yard. "Children, there is an elk out there," he said to us still looking out the south facing kitchen window.

"Ya," said my oldest brother Anton, "there is an elephant on the roof of the workshop as well!"

We were used to Dad exaggerating at times. He kidded us a lot in order to get our attention. We were not sure if Dad was kidding or not, so we ran to the kitchen window to see for ourselves. Most of the windowpanes were frosted with a layer of ice caused by condensation, often forming the most beautiful and fascinating ice flowers. There were some small centers of the windowpanes where the ice was clear enough to see through, so we scrambled to look through them. However, the distorted vision showed an elk twice the normal length and the antlers twice as wide as normal. It was a big animal - almost as big as a cow, with well-endowed shoulders and a round rump, and a long shiny coat.

We quickly put on our winter clothes and boots and went outside, to see if we could corner the elk. In the meantime, the elk slowly sauntered up to the east side of our property where there was a small clump of fifteen year-old spruce trees, about a hundred of them. Opa Anton had planted these trees.

Our property was partly fenced with a live spruce hedge and a post and plank fence. On the south side of our property, the creek was the natural borderline as the shrubs, bushes and tree branches were laden with ice from the steaming creek water that glittered in the rays of the sun.

Michael Lang was a short, lean and wiry man, with a well-tanned face and always had an infectious smile. He was on the road outside the fence when he spotted the elk. Michael was on his way to the flourmill where he worked. He very quickly pulled out one of the snow and ditch markers beside the road. This marker was at least two meters in length. Then, he climbed through our plank fence and used the marker as a tool to herd the elk back towards our house, some three hundred meters to the west. He did this in a relaxed manner and with a calm soothing voice, which the elk seemed to respond to. The elk came towards us quite tamely and when it was about halfway, Michael yelled for us open the garden gate.

Our vegetable garden was big, big enough for at least twenty elks. To keep the unwanted animals out of the veggie patch during the growing season Dad had built a two-meter high chain link fence with a meter wide gate facing our house. Dad went quickly to it, but the garden gate was frozen in its place. He finally wiggled it a little and then, with tremendous force, he lifted it out of its hinges. It came out with a huge clump of snow and ice attached at the bottom. There were even some icy clumps of grass still attached. Dad leaned the gate on the garden fence, some three meters away from the gateposts.

Michael continued to herd the elk into this garden. In the meantime, we tried to block the elk's escape route. A dozen of our neighbors came out to help. They appeared dressed in their pajamas, felt boots, and heavy coats thrown over it all and topped off with some woolen tuques. My older brothers Hans and Rudi were very athletic and quickly climbed the huge stack of neatly piled one-by-six oak boards that were right under the extended roof of Dad's workshop. The boards had been carefully piled up with cross strips to prevent them from twisting and warping, while curing and drying. The boys quickly handed down the boards to the waiting neighbors. Within minutes, everyone was ready with sticks and boards, and whatever else we could find. We stood side by side in a line and barricaded the escape route that the elk had used to come onto our property.

High tension and excitement was in the air. The elk got a bit nervous seeing so many people. It came to a stop, finally facing the garden gate. Comments from some neighbors included, "Elk meat is the best," and "Salami time!"

They were dreaming in the middle of the day, as meat was very scarce and very expensive. These people did not come for the fun of the chase alone. They were seriously expecting to get some share of the meat. We had the elk surrounded, and it tried to escape into the garden. Obviously, the elk was familiar with chain link fencing, as it was not scared of it. It tried many times to get through the garden gate but could not. His crown was just too big… it even tried twisting its head sideways but still couldn't get through.

Finally, the elk gave up and bolted past Michael narrowly missing him. The elk continued to run at a good speed and jumped the creek with ease and ended up in the dense forest of our neighbor's property. All we could hear for a short while was crashing and snapping of twigs and dry branches.

Even after the elk was gone, about fifteen adults and ten children remained, debating about the elk and what a good elk roast it would have been. Mr. Aichsteiner, one of the neighbors, stated that something must have been wrong with this animal, as this was a very unusual occurrence. He also mentioned that in a different region of the Alps, some chamois were found dead, low in the valleys in the wintertime. When the vet dissected the carcasses he found that these animals were severely sick from a parasite in their blood stream, caused by a fly that had laid its eggs into an open wound or nostrils.

The following week, a story appeared in the local newspaper describing that some vandals had cut the wire fence of a private and enclosed elk habitat that belonged to the local cement mill owner Mr. Ritter. Mr. Ritter offered a large sum of money, five hundred German Marks, for information as to the exact whereabouts of the runaway elk. A speedy capture of the animal was paramount. Special posters announcing the reward were also nailed to the church doors in all villages within a thirty-kilometer radius of Mr. Ritter's elk habitat. We calculated that the elk we had seen had only been roaming free for one night when it arrived on our property.

One day after the reward was posted, on a lightly snowing day, four children on their way to school in the village of Riedering, about seven kilometers to the north of our home, reported to their teacher Frau Reichel that they had seen a big elk at a distance.

The newspaper announced that over two hundred people were ready to volunteer in capturing the elk. The cement mill's Fire Captain was appointed to be in charge of transporting these volunteers to the final round up, with trucks and buses belonging to the cement plant. Also, long sections of old World War II camouflaged netting was rolled up and stacked on the trucks. This was a serious operation; after all, this was a huge amount of money being offered, with an expiry time of four weeks from the original posted date. The hunt excited a lot of people and they became eager to keep a look out for the elk on their own. Quite a number of tough men and women from the surrounding countryside started following tracks in their spare time, suspecting that any hoof prints were from the elk, but due to the additional snowfall, they were not very clear.

Within the first week, two snowfalls increased the snow depth by another fifteen centimeters. Some trackers used skis or even constructed snowshoes that they had seen illustrated in adventure books by Karl Mai, where North American native Indians walked with these contraptions on the snow.

The local chimney sweep, Fritz Aulinger, was involved in the search for the elk. He was a lean, tall, lanky man who was as agile as a cat, and had on several occasions fallen off the roofs where he was working and had never been injured. He would just get up and climb back on the roof again to continue his work. When tracking the elk he devised a system to eliminate his tracks in the snow by pulling a bundle of spruce branches on a rope behind him. He successfully erased his own tracks and that of the elk.

Soon there were others who copied Fritz's system of eliminating their tracks so that others could not follow. For example, someone like Jack Meixner, who was known to let the women on his small farm do the hard work, while he found the easy chores. Trackers were afraid of being spied on and outwitted by such characters like Jack Meixner who could possibly claim the reward with minimum effort, at the very last minute. Two such people were seen on a clear full moon night, following some tracker's tracks and they were known to come from the neighboring village of Sollhuben.

The excitement grew, and more and more people joined in the search. Chances were great that the elk could come across your trail. At one point, the elk was resting and chewing its cud in between cluster of small three-meter trees. It had snowed heavily during the night. The elk was very comfortable and warm with its coat and antlers covered with a snow blanket. It suddenly stopped chewing and perked its ears. The elk could hear a faint swoosh, swoosh, swoosh. The trackers Walter and Laura Waldinger went by so very close on their skis - only ten meters away - and did not see the animal. Somehow the elk must have sensed that there was no dog with the Waldinger's or it would have jumped up in a hurry and run.

At Neuners Bakery, in the town of Höhenmoos, Mrs. Kustermann, the local piano teacher, was very excited. She told other shoppers that she had seen the great big elk, the day before, right outside her kitchen window. The animal had seen its reflection in the window and then touched the glass with its wet nose, thinking that there was another elk. Then, it calmly walked away.

Mr. Erwin Strohbach, the schoolteacher at the village of Wangen, had a great idea how to make some money out of this exciting development. He bought an official map of the region, then made rough copies of the local area with carbon paper. He titled these maps: "THE ELK IS GUARANTEED IN THIS REGION" and supplied the grocery stores in the area with them. These rough maps sold extremely well and Mr. Strohbach had a really hard time keeping up with the demand. The grocery stores and Mr. Strohbach made good money with these maps. The price was a steep 4 Marks each and he sold two hundred and forty four copies. The trackers used these maps to find out where they were and then studied their route to accurately hunt the elk. They used all kinds of different breeds of dogs to follow the trail of tracks that they thought were made by the elk in question. Naturally, most of these dogs were not ideally suited for or even trained to follow a scent. Squirrels and rabbits and other small animals distracted them, plus there were many older animal tracks that were partially snowed over, many of which ended abruptly at creeks.

On the fifteenth day of the chase, Mr. Ritter increased the reward for a successful capture of the elk, to the sum of one thousand German Marks plus fifty sacks of cement! He expanded the notices another ten kilometers in all directions outside the former boundary. These notices were posted outside all church and municipal announcement boards.

The gossip everywhere, including the local beer pub, the grocery store, the millwright, the flourmill, and the blacksmith's was exclusively about the roaming elk and its reward. Leonard Spiegel, the pub owner, explained to his guests that in Oberaudorf, the value of the trophy antlers would be at least five hundred Marks. These horns could be carved into traditional costume buttons and they themselves bring in lots of money. For example, two seven centimeter base crowns with edelweiss nicely carved into them as the center decoration for the hosentraeger or suspenders for leather pants, could be sold for at least one hundred and eighty Marks alone. The meat would bring in over one thousand Marks on the black market or probably even more if sold to a gourmet restaurant like Feinschmecker's in Munich. Some of Leonard's guests listened carefully to those with beer-loosened tongues and tried to zero in on the elk's location, in hopes of cornering it and claiming the reward.

Farmer Christian Wacker, in Rathhausen, told the blacksmith Sep Mauser, that the elk had been pulling out hay from his hayshed. He made a point of emphasizing that the elk enjoyed his high quality clover hay. But, by the time he arrived, there was no elk in sight, only lots of tracks. In fact, there were so many tracks, that it appeared that there were two elks roaming around. He boasted that it was guaranteed that this elk would be back for more hay and all he had to do was wait for the elk to return. This caused some of the adventurers to secretly hide in the hayshed hoping that the elk would return.

The following night, another ten centimeters of snow fell on the whole area.

There were devious clowns amongst the beer pub patrons, who spread false information. As a result, on Saturday afternoon, eleven men and four of their wives arrived at a meadow on the other side of the Inn River, looking for the elusive elk. They found a lot of horse tracks visible in the snow, but no elk. Slowly, after a few days, some of the people gave up the search – either they were unable to find any leads or they figured out that they had been mislead.

In reality people were searching almost twenty kilometers to the west of where the elk was. An additional snowfall made the search a lot harder. By now the elk had been out of the enclosure for about three weeks. Mailman Georg Stetler went downhill on his cross-country skies once a week, on a delivery run to our Dad's cousin Anderl and Theresa Neumond in the village of Grainbach. He was so surprised when he almost collided with the elk that he nearly lost all his mail. He told his friend Tobias Lederer about his near collision with the elk. As the mailman was very fond of talking and spreading the word Tobias made him promise that he would keep the secret to himself for another three days before he could divulge the whereabouts of the elk to anyone else.

To further increase the excitement, some beer pub owners went so far as to even take bets as to whether the elk would be captured alive, if it would disappear in someone's roasting pot or if the elk would make its way up hill to join the roaming herd of wild elk.

The high-pitched church bell rang the noon hour and a slight breeze carried the sound faintly over the Farmer Seidl's meadow. It was just at this time that local hunter Theodor Braunnickel, owner of a very big farm and a huge gravel pit near the city of Munich, was by the Prien Creek checking out his fox and the smaller martin traps, when he came up the ravine and into the meadow. He looked to the east and saw to his disbelief that a huge lone trophy elk was feeding calmly at farmer Seidl's hay shed – only some 80 meters away. In his past, he had missed a few opportunities to bag a good trophy deer simply because he was too slow. Braunnickel was aware that the season for hunting elk was long past. He realized that now, if he wanted to bag this very big trophy elk, he just had to be quicker! And no one would know, if he was quick about it. He calmly took the gun from his shoulder, moved the safety lever, aimed, and BANG! The elk was his!!

No one would have known it if it wasn't for Tobias Lederer. He was one of the volunteer trackers who happened to be very close on the heels of the elk. With the help of his fox terrier Woidl, he had crossed the elk's tracks for the fourth time that day. It was snowing lightly. Tobias was just at the edge of the forest - only a hundred meters away from where the elk was feeding. It was pulling out some of the aromatic hay from between the horizontal slat boards of the hay shed in the middle of the meadow. (This was about sixteen kilometers away from the village where we lived). Tobias heard the muffled echo of a gunshot, and then he saw the elk collapse. As you can imagine, Tobias was stunned and his heart missed a beat. He picked up his fox terrier Woidl

to make sure that he did not bark. Three days of tracking the elk and now what? Tobias waited a while for the
marksman to come to the collapsed elk.

Tobias realized that he had lost his reward of one
thousand German Marks. He figured that the next best
thing was to share the meat with the hunter equally.
With new resolve, Tobias waited another little while and
then went out into the meadow and over to the farmers hayshed where he found the over-under 9mm Sauer
gun, an elaborate Zeiss 7X50 binoculars and a hunter's
rucksack. They were secured to a wooden peg on the
corner post of the hayshed, a place intended for the
farmers scythe.

Tobias saw that a man with a full beard was very busy
butchering the elk. He very bluntly said to him, "Was
it necessary to kill that tame elk that had an aluminum
tag in his left ear?" It was Mr. Braunnickel the hunter. He
was actually not aware of any missing elk or the reward
money since he lived out of the area but he did have a
hunting license for this particular area.

With a very a red face, bulging eyes and with a very
loud voice he ordered Tobias to, "Go and get lost."
Just then, a gust of wind blew some snow off the roof
of the hay shed, onto Tobias's back, and then finally
landed on Braunnickel's face and upper body. It was
almost a sign that the spirits were not happy with his
deed and this did not make the situation any better.
Tobias argued back to Mr. Braunnickel that because of

his irresponsible and blatant killing of a tame animal, he had lost his reward and therefore he was entitled to half of the meat.

Mr. Braunnickel yelled at and threatened Tobias. While he pointed at him with the bloody knife he continued to butcher the elk.

"Okay, have it your way." Tobias left and went to the nearest Farmhouse, a kilometer away. He told the farmer's wife, Mrs. Seidl, what was happening. She informed Tobias that her husband was half way up Schwarzberg Mountain, cutting trees for timber. So, Tobias left his dog Woidl at the farm, where the children were delighted to play with him, and borrowed a horse to ride to the next village. The only horse the farmer had was a Clysdale horse, a huge animal not used of being ridden. Just to have to get on the horse and ride bareback was very scary as he was not used to riding horses. Tobias secured the reins, and then climbed on the half door in the stable where the horse was kept in order to be able to mount the animal. One of the boys opened the barn gate and the horse finally moved, almost knocking Tobias off at the gatepost.

Tobias was definitely not an experienced rider. He tried everything he could to make the horse go faster and finally succeeded by pulling and twisting on the horse's mane. This made it jump and it galloped at full speed across the meadow, across a small frozen pond, and headed for the police station. Tobias had to hang on for dear life. In the end, he flung himself from the horse onto a high snow pile so that he did not get himself trampled to death.

Fred Kink, the junior policeman, had just finished shoveling the snow off the roadway. Fred had grown up on a farm and knew how to handle horses. He retrieved the horse and tied him up. After Tobias brushed the snow off himself, he went inside the police station where it was nice and cozy warm. The first thing he did was to ask to have an urgent call put through to the cement plant owner, Mr. Ritter.

The policeman on duty was very polite and complied immediately. He reckoned that some of the reward money could possibly end up at the police station. When Mr. Ritter was on the line, Tobias explained what had happened, but of course, only told half of the story. Mr. Ritter told Tobias that he will handle the situation and not to worry. Mr. Ritter then ordered the policeman to arrest the hunter immediately and that he would be there in a half an hour, with his chauffeur and some more policemen from the next bigger detachment.

Theodor Braunnickel, the hunter, was arrested and charged for hunting out of season. The meat was donated to the nearest orphanage. Two months later, the judge fined Mr. Braunnickel the sum of two hundred German Marks for violating the district hunting regulations. Mr. Braunnickel's lawyer argued in Court that, "In the past, if there ever was an elk so low in the valley in the winter time, the animal was suspected of being sick, and according to the Ministry of Forest's hunting regulation, sick wild animals must be destroyed." So, the two hundred German Mark fine was dropped.

Mr. Ritter kept the elk's trophy horns and had them specially mounted above the balcony of his villa. The hide was turned into leather hosen (pants) and auctioned off with the proceeds going to the local orphanage. Tobias got a handshake, with many thanks from Mr. Ritter, and a load of cement anytime in the future if he ever decided to build a house. Four years later, Tobias moved into his new home with his new wife Alexandra. The new Mr. and Mrs. Lederer had happily made use of all that cement.

CHAPTER 30

PETER HOCHMUELLER

On one of our summer hiking trails in 1949, we passed by the Hochmueller's farmhouse where the grand-daughter Creszenzia was running the operation of the farm. She managed a variety of milk cows and had a healthy stand of fruit trees on the hillside, thanks to her great grandparents, grandparents and parents who had planted some fruit trees every year and replaced the diseased trees as well as the old ones. This resulted in a respectable sized healthy orchard.

This story is mainly about the old Grandpa Peter, who was in his mid eighties at the time that we met him. He was a tall man, had not lost any of his blond hair and was still quite agile, but yes, he had slowed down a bit. He was known to be a very honorable and con-scientious honest man. Peter was chosen many times for jury duty. His sideline was to assist the District Land Surveyors. Peter, therefore, was very knowledgeable about the location of surveyor markers. He was eventu-ally sworn in as an advisor to the District Land Office. Consequently, in many land survey disputes, Peter's opinion carried a lot of weight in court.

This is the extraordinary story he told us this day.

In April 1916, Peter was busy plowing the soil for the field that he had planned. He calculated that his strong team of two oxen could complete the job in about two days.

At about 2 p.m., while Peter was following the plow, he was hit on his left shoulder by a sharp object. All he could feel was a hard slap and he almost fell forward. He felt no pain at that moment just a slight sting. Immediately he reached up and explored his left shoulder with his right hand. He felt that a hard object had gone through his jacket, shirt and into the muscle. The lump on his shoulder worried him so he calmly unhitched the oxen from the plough and left them so that they could wander over to the grassy area and nibble a bit.

He went home and Mrs. Hochmueller helped him remove his jacket and shirt to investigate the situation. She said, "It looks as if a bullet is partly imbedded in your shoulder!" She ordered him to sit down on a chair as she suspected that he might faint. She went to get a bottle of arnica ointment and then went to the tool shed and retrieved an ancient pair of long handled forge pliers.

Mrs. Hochmueller liberally applied the arnica ointment on his shoulder and gave Peter a clean rolled up handkerchief for him to bite into. She then attempted to grab the exposed bullet with the forge pliers. However, the forge pliers were a little bit too big. She quickly went back into her living room and retrieved from her sewing basket a small piece of leather that she inserted into the pliers' mouth. Now she was ready to grab the bullet as it held well. With great force, she pushed the open pliers against Peter's shoulder and then with the left hand she kept pressure and with the right hand she closed the pliers. Once she had a grip on the bullet, she turned the pliers and yanked the bullet out.

Until that moment, the wound had not bled much. But without the bullet in the shoulder, it all of a sudden started to bleed a lot. Peter put his handkerchief over the wound while Mrs. Hochmueller got some bandages and more ointment and applied them right away.

When all this was done and the bleeding stopped, Peter got dressed and went out to the field to finish his plowing for the day.

It healed very well and quickly. The news of Peter's mishap spread mainly through the mailman who made his regular rounds in this community. Peter now could brag about the stray bullet for a long time. He kept the bullet, jacked and shirt with the hole in them as evidence, as many of his friends and relatives wanted to see it to believe it! Peter considered himself to be a very lucky person to be alive.

A local newspaper reporter got to hear about Peter's story and he did some further research. He came to the conclusion that, at the time of the incident, a local wedding was taking place in the neighboring village of Schauraing whereby boisterous family members celebrated by making loud noises with gunshots in the air. One of these bullets is most probably what hit Peter!

Dad's Bug Story

or

Mrs. Schneemann

CHAPTER 31

DAD'S BUG STORY

(This story was Dad's favorite and he told it many times over to all his friends and we children listened carefully to it until we knew the whole story by heart!)

In contrast to the regular country folk of the area, the Schneemann's were a flamboyant and colorful couple. Mrs. Kunigunde Schneemann was a very sophisticated lady whose husband was at least twenty-five years her senior. She was very lively and loved to dress in the latest fashions. She especially loved to show off her very fashionable large hats.

Mr. Wilfried Schneemann had white hair which he combed straight back. He stood out as an exquisitely and expensively dressed man. When he walked every day, he walked with his torso very erect, while swinging his horn cane. With every step he took, he stabbed the air. He was a quiet man who did not speak very much, so it was hard for the local folks to get to know him, even though they encountered him on his daily walks in the countryside. All that was known of Mr. Schneemann was that he was a diplomat in the service of the German

Kaiser Wilhelm and had been posted to Stockholm, Sweden, as Consul for most of his career.

At his retirement, the Schneemanns bought a secluded estate with ten hectares of farmland plus three and a half hectares of timber in the Alpine region, nearly 80 km south east of Munich. However, in 1933, to their great surprise, the Third Reich built the "Munich-Salzburg" autobahn right through the middle of their property. The Schneemanns were financially very well compensated for their loss of land and according to the local mailman Walter Zetl, they were able to considerably increase the worth of their bank accounts in Zurich.

Unfortunately, in 1940, Mr. Schneemann died at the age of 82. This left Mrs. Schneemann alone to look after her estate, so she hired a farm helper called Blasius Bretschneider. However, in July 1942, Blasius was drafted to the eastern war front and only four weeks later, was declared missing in action. A month later, Mrs. Schneemann was allocated a Russian POW farm helper named Yussef Pedrofsky. He seemed to be a well-educated man of about 32 years of age.

Yussef adapted quickly and did his best to get along with the local people. Mrs. Schneemann considered herself very lucky to have Yussef working for her. At first, she communicated with him in French, but Yussef insisted on learning German. He was also a very talented artist oil painter and in his little spare time, he produced a number of oil paintings that he sold cheap to some of Mrs. Schneemann's friends who had an eye for good art.

Mrs. Schneemann raised sheep as a hobby and had acquired some excellent breeding stock from East Friesland. These sheep were very hardy, larger than average sized sheep, with magnificent wool. They had black heads and black feet while the rest of their coat was pure white. All her rams and sheep were marked on the ears with brass tags that were stamped and numbered by the Ministry of Agriculture. As they were pure breed, the rams fetched a good price at farm auctions and her stud fees were exorbitantly high. Most of her customers were well to do sheep farmers who came from far away with their ewes.

Occasionally, some of the rams escaped and would eventually join other local farmer's sheep in pastures that were kilometers away. These farmers would keep the rams for a few extra days before returning them to Mrs. Schneemann. She was very pleased to get her rams back so she rewarded them very generously with gifts of her very expensive, good quality schnapps. Of course, six months later there were additions of black-headed lambs in these farmer's flocks.

One day, Mrs. Schneemann and Mr. Meindel the baker, had an argument while standing in line at the local grocery store. They were waiting to purchase their allotted amount of sugar with the food stamps they had been given by the local government. The sugar they were waiting for came straight from the sugar factory near Passau. It was derived from sugar beets so it was amber in color and had a strong taste of molasses.

There was a long line-up of customers who were waiting for the sugar to be delivered from the railway to the grocery store by horse and cart. Mr. Meindel had been waiting awhile and was the eighth person in the line when Mrs. Schneemann arrived. Ignoring those waiting in line, she went straight to the front. She considered it a degrading thing to have to wait in line anywhere. In fact, under normal circumstances, Mrs. Schneemann would not have even gone to the store, but rather would have sent her maid Liesel to do her shopping. Liesel though, had been drafted into working for the war effort and was working at a factory in the outskirts of the city of Rosenheim, making bullet casings.

When Mrs. Schneemann got to the front of the line where Mrs. Applewood was standing, she said in a dominating voice, "You don't mind if I join you!" It was not a question. Mrs. Applewood was a small, frail lady, well into her seventies. Her dachshund dog Susi barked at Mrs. Schneemann, but Mrs. Applewood herself did not like to have any attention drawn to her, so she just nodded her head in agreement to avoid confrontation.

Mr. Meindel, the baker, was a righteous man and did not agree with Mrs. Schneemann's pushiness. He was tall and in good shape for his sixty-seven years. In his spare time, he was also the director of the local men's choir. In a booming baritone voice he sang out to the melody of Karl Zeller's "der Vogelhandler" (the bird merchant):

"Mrs. Schneemann can't get in the line
Like all the other citizens
But it would be good for her
To take the last spot where she belongs
Haissa tra la la......"

For a moment, the crowd was silent. Then they suddenly started cheering and applauding. Under her elaborate hat, Mrs. Schneemann's face became beet red as she glared at Mr. Meindel. She huffed and went meekly to the back of the line. From then on, she vowed to get even with Mr. Meindel whenever she could.

One rainy day in October, about a year later, Mrs. Schneemann noticed a dark spot in her slice of rye bread. With the tip of her bread knife, she carefully extracted a well-cooked black bug in the baked loaf. Of course, she blamed the baker. "I will get even with you Mr. Meindel and humble you once and for all" she mumbled to herself.

She went to the telephone mounted on the wall in her office. A telephone in those days was a luxury item and only four households in the village had them. She turned the crank handle vigorously and asked the operator to connect her to the local Police Station.

Sergeant Fritz Unrau answered the call. He had his office in Wangen, which was the next village some 10 kilometers up the valley. Fritz Unrau was a tall skinny man with hazel eyes, ears a tad larger than normal and they stood out a little forward so when he spoke, it appeared that his ears were moving. It was comical to witness and consequently, hard to keep a straight face when having a conversation with him. He spoke slowly so you had the urge to help him along by guessing what he was going to say. He also had a sleepy look in his eyes, as his eyelids were always quarter down, even when he looked up in the sky. Under his green uniform cap, he had a reddish bristle crew cut.

Fritz Unrau was responsible for an area that covered seven villages. He believed that his workload was too heavy and that this could cause him to have a shorter lifespan. He used every trick in the book to conserve his precious energy. His life philosophy was to do as little as possible at home or at the office

Once connected to Sergeant Unrau, Mrs. Schneemann screeched in an elevated voice: "This is to register an official complaint... a police report is required." Sgt. Unrau was not at all impressed that she was demanding that he had to fill in a report. This was a lot of work, as they had to be filled out in quadruplicate! One copy was to be sent to the city of Rosenheim, to his superior, the nasty Inspector Arnold Klopp who always found some mistake or fault. Klopp purposely belittled the lower ranking members of the District, as he believed that they needed to be put in their places in order to be able to recognize his superiority. The second copy was to be sent to the District Sanitary and Health Department and the third copy was for the complainant, Mrs. Schneemann, and finally the forth copy was for his own file.

Still on the phone, Mrs. Schneemann demanded that Sergeant Fritz Unrau immediately get on his bicycle and pedal to her house to collect the evidence. She demanded that he had to make a report and secure the unsanitary bug that she had found in the loaf of bread that she had purchased that day from baker Meindel's Bakerei, as evidence. If it would have been anyone else, the Sgt. would have told them that he was way too busy and that he would look into it at the earliest opportunity, maybe the following week, when enough time had passed for things to settle down. But with Mrs. Schneemann, there was no escape. If he didn't respond, she would have him reported to the nasty Inspector Klopp very quickly and possible by phone.

On his way down the hill from his office to Mrs. Schneemann's house, the Sgt. pondered the likelihood of being rewarded for his immediate response with a good meal and maybe a glass of Schnapps. After all, Mrs. Schneemann was known to be rather generous if she wanted to. He glanced at his government issued Heinzmann pocket-watch and it indicated that it was 11.05 a.m. - just in time for lunch.

Finally, Sergeant Unrau finished his report and sent it by railway on the 4:45 p.m. train. The bug was safely enclosed in a big one-liter glass jam jar, complete with a snap on lid and rubber seal ring. He sealed the jar and locked it in a white canvass mailbag addressed to the District Sanitary and Health Department, and marked it with a yellow and black striped express tag.

One week later, Mrs. Shillink the food Inspector, arrived at Meindel's bakery at precisely 8 a.m. opening time. Mrs. Shillink was a very stern and humorless woman in her early fifties, with long gray hair that she wore in a bun at the back of her neck. Mr. Meindel was not happy to see her.

After an extra long and thorough inspection of everything, Mrs. Shillink handed baker Meindel a writ from the District Sanitary and Health Department. He had to appear at the Courthouse on Saline Strasse 14, to explain to the Court why there was an unsanitary bug, the size of a common ladybug, the color of tar, in one of his products that he had sold to Mrs. Schneemann on November 20th, 1942. He had to appear before the judge or his bakery would be closed down.

Mr. Meindel arrived by bicycle at the Courthouse at precisely 9:50 a.m. He had already finished his day's work. He had started mixing his dough and baking bread at 3 a.m. that morning. In the courtroom, Police Sergeant Fritz Unrau had also arrived. For once his normally rumpled uniform was ironed and clean, his khaki shirt starched, his black tie ironed, and his boots polished and shone like never before.

Mrs. Schneemann had arrived by train. She sat smugly with Sergeant Unrau in the witness section, waiting for the court proceedings to begin, gleefully anticipating Meindel's demise. Mrs. Schneemann had brought her husband's special 20X1 Zeiss office magnifying glass. It was in a forteen carat gold filigree case that had an engraved ivory handle attached to it. Her husband had made great use of this magnifying glass identifying fake documents. Just in case the shortsighted Judge had trouble identifying the bug or the sly Mr. Meindel came up with some tricks, Mrs. Schneemann was prepared to lend it to the Judge.

Inspector Shillink was dressed in a snow-white overcoat. She removed the bug from the glass jar and placed it onto a white sheet of paper marked "EVIDENCE" in large printed block letters. There appeared to be some dog hair in the jar presumably from Mrs. Schneemann's dog. A vain woman, Mrs. Shillink did not like to put on her glasses in public and did not want to advertise that her eyesight was diminishing. She blew the suspected dog hair off the paper, off the desk and onto the floor. Mrs. Shillink put the paper beside Sergeant Unrau's official police report on the judge's desk.

At 10 a.m., on the last chime of the huge court clock, Judge Simon Berg arrived in the courtroom. The judge was an elderly gentleman who wore extremely strong glasses, had bushy eyebrows and a large purplish bulbous nose. He was very serious and looked annoyed. As he walked in he was flicking off some real or imaginary dog hair off his black court robe. Judge Berg had been transferred from Heidelberg two years prior. At the time, civil servants could not be demoted because of habitual excessive indulgences. Instead, they were transferred to another place. Today, Judge Simon Berg was not in a good mood. His predawn migraine headaches had robbed him of his final three hours of sleep. He planned to deal with his cases that day as swiftly and harshly as possible, so he could relax in the afternoon.

The court secretary, Mr. Freitak, was a short man with a Charlie Chaplin moustache and an oversized Adam's apple that moved vigorously up and down when he talked. His voice was squeaky and high pitched when he commanded everyone to raise and stand at attention for the arrival of the judge.

Mr. Freitak screamed "Heil Hitler" and everyone raised their right hand and shouted "Heil Hitler" while saluting the Fuhrer's portrait - a sixty by ninety centimeter picture mounted on the wall behind the Judge's bench under the clock. Only Mr. Meindel said "drei liter" (three liters) while he saluted. Fortunately, no one noticed, as he could have gotten into a lot of trouble.

The judge declared the court in session and asked police Sergeant Fritz Unrau to come forward to identify the evidence and verify his report. Next, Mrs. Schneemann was asked to come forward by the court clerk. She had to state her name, address and where the bug was found, including the date and precise time. After Mrs. Schneemann, the District Sanitary and Health Inspector was called forward to verify the inspection report she had written.

Finally, the court secretary asked the accused, Mr. Robert Meindel, baker in Muehlwang, to come forward, state his name, address and occupation. Mr. Meindel raised his right hand - with thumb, index and middle finger extended, ring finger and pinkie curled inwards, and he stated that he swore to tell the truth and nothing but the truth.

Following German court customs, the judge read the report loud and clear and then asked Mr. Meindel "What have you got to say to that?"

Mr. Meindel moved slowly up to the judge's desk where the bug was displayed on the white sheet of paper. By now, with all the handling, the wings and legs of the bug had fallen off and were missing. Mr. Meindel took a closer look. He very calmly reached over the desk, took the bug between his fingers smelt it and put it in his mouth, chewed and swallowed it. "Mmmmm......," he said, "That was a raisin!"

There was absolute silence in the courtroom for a long minute. "Well," said the Judge, "if that was a raisin and you'll swear to it, then this case is dismissed!" With that, he banged his gavel on his desk and closed the proceedings.

In that moment, Mrs. Schneemann who could not suppress her disbelief, let out a high pitched "Naa."

The judge glared at her and warned her that further outbursts would land her in jail. In a loud voice, he reminded everyone that he was in charge in the court-room. Mrs. Schneemann humbly apologized and the Judge let it go at that. The court secretary cleared the room for the next case to be heard.

For many years afterwards, his friends teased Mr. Meindel, the baker. They enjoyed asking him, "Now Robert, was the bug very sweet? Or was the raisin very crunchy?" He always answered, "It was the best raisin I ever had!"

They had a good laugh and raised their glasses to good health. And because his friends were all in the men's choir, they sang:

"Haissa tra la la! Fide ra la la, fide ra la la, fide ra
la la la la
Frau Schneemann kann sich nicht stellen an
Wie alle anderen Buergerlein
Doch waere es recht fuer sie geziemt
Und das hintere Platzchen nimmt
Haissa tralala."

"Frau Scheemann cannot get in line like all the other citizens
But it suits her best if she would take her proper spot
At the back of the line..
Haissa Tra la la! Fide ra la la, fide ra la la, fide ra
la la la la."

CHAPTER 32

MODE OF TRANSPORTATION

My brother Rudi was 4 years older than I and was the first of the boys to leave home to take up an apprenticeship. On September 1, 1951, he became a tool and dye maker at a very large company called Sluter Manufacturing. Sluter Manufacturing was in the town of Friesing, about 150 kilometers from our home so Rudi had to travel by train to get there. While in Friesing, Rudi would need a bicycle to get to and from the monastery dormitory and the factory because, even at a brisk walk, it would take Rudi about 45 minutes to get to work.

The Christian brothers at the nearby monastery in Friesing, provided food and accommodation for about sixty young apprentices working at the various factories in town. Mom had to pay a fee of a hundred and fifty German Marks per month for Rudi's accommodation, which was a lot of money in those days. But somehow, I think that Opa paid for it because there was no way that Mom and Dad could afford that much money.

On the first week of July, on a beautiful sunny Sunday morning, when the birds were chirping noisily in the shady trees, our family was out on a hiking trail in the mountain area. We passed by some very old farmhouses.

Dad was a very social person and loved to chat with everyone on the trail. Shortly after we began our hike, we passed by some very old farmhouses and ran into a farmer by the name of Melchior Fischer. Melchior had a bicycle standing in his open farm machinery shed, so Dad inquired if the bicycle was for sale.

"Well.......," Melchior answered in a very slow dragged out way. "Maybe....." Dad asked if it worked. Melchior again answered, "Maybe.... The last time it worked was before the war."

The bicycle had a good quality frame, made by the Adler Company. It had a very small forty cubic centimeter helper motor attached to the frame behind the seat. The tires were solid and had been made from hundreds of five-centimeter diameter punched out plugs from old car tires. These plugs were strung together through the center hole with a strong wire to create a tire. Dad tested the bike. First he checked it's pedal power, and then he checked if there was any fuel in the helper motor tank.

Melchior went into his house and shortly after came back out with a candle and matches. He lit the candle, held it over the gas tank and looked into it. We all jumped back expecting the tank to blow up, but nothing happened. Dad realized that if there was no gasoline, he could not check if the motor was working. So he offered Melchior twenty marks for the bicycle and Melchior readily accepted. Naturally, Dad did not have the money on him so we went home to get it. Right away, we went back up hill to Melchior's farm and gave him his money. Rudi peddled it home.

At home, Dad removed the motor and took it to the local mechanic by the name of Albert Rehl. Albert took the carburetor apart, cleaned it out and reassembled it, and got the little motor working. He also reinstalled it back on the bicycle. Rudi's bike was ready to go.

Albert also sold gasoline from a gas pump. The pump had a ten-liter glass tube on top of it that had a black mark indicating the fuel level for every half-liter. It also had a handle on the side to pump the gasoline up to the tube. Dad ordered some gas for the bike. Mr. Rehl pumped the handle left and right and the gasoline went up into the glass tube. Then he turned a valve and the gasoline flowed into the bike's gas tank.

To use the helper motor, you had to pull the lever at the handle bar, which activated the clutch while ped-dling, and it would engage the motor and pull the bike. The only drawback was that those hard tires made it very uncomfortable to ride on a gravel road. Rudi was very pleased to be in possession of this bicycle and took it with him by train to Friesing. There he used it over the next two and a half years to get to work and back.

Then, unfortunately, one day someone broke the bike's lock and stole it right from the workers bike lot. Rudi was very mad at the thief. We all felt sorry for him. Without a bike Rudi had to walk a long way in the morning and the same in the evening, until he had enough money saved to buy himself a second hand regular bicycle.

CHAPTER 33

THE HAGEN'S

In 1952, Mrs. Schuster (the mailman's widow), passed away at the age of 89. They had no relatives. Their quaint Bavarian house, with its overhanging roof and lots of beautiful red geraniums on the balcony, was auctioned off by the District Land Office to a couple who had just arrived from Miami. Their names were Mr. and Mrs. Hagen.

Mr. Hagen was in his mid forties and had an athletic body, but he was completely bald. He weighed about eighty kilos and was average tall. Mrs. Hagen was a short, plump, lady with dark hair, who was also very energetic.

They were both constantly working on their house, even on Sundays. According to the local Priest, this was a major sin.

They hired some young teenagers to do odd jobs around the house, and I was one of them. The jobs included digging and chiselling inside the house walls in order to install new wiring tubes. The major digging was done in the basement and in the garden area. They never paid our salary in cash, instead they paid us in used clothing that was still in reasonably good condition. The clothes never fitted right – they were way too big and needed to be altered by the tailor.

The local tailor was a refugee from Berlin. His name was Kort. We never knew whether Kort was his family name or his Christian name. Kort lived in a portable, temporary shelter with a large dog. Whenever we picked up the clothes that he had altered, we were sure they would fit us perfectly as he was that good of a tailor. The only downside was that we had to wait a month to six weeks and sometimes even longer for him to finish his work and our clothes were always covered with long dog hair. We suspected that the dog used our clothes to sleep on! But none the less, he was a great tailor and very reasonable in what he charged us.

Mr. and Mrs. Hagen seemed to be paranoid with the fear of fire and were determined to put fire escapes everywhere that was possible. He took his time to explain to us boys that fire was a very serious thing. In Miami, where he had been living, houses would burn down within minutes and many people perished in these house fires.

The first fire escape we helped to put in, was up in the attic. As you opened the huge roof window, a fireproof ladder would automatically deploy. There was also a flexible steel cable coil installed above the window, that could be used to let yourself down and get out quickly. Both of the Hagen's tested this fire exit many times and even checked their speed with a stop watch to see how long it took them to get out.

The most mysterious fire escape was the one in his cellar. He expanded his cellar by making it twice as big as it normally was. Then he added an underground tunnel, that was some eighteen meters long and ended up inside the garden shed at the back of the property. The tunnel was not very big so you had to crawl down on your hands and knees to get to the other end. This wasn't fast enough, so Mr. Hagen installed a mechanic's low wheel dolly that, when you removed a pin, it would silently pull you down to the garden shed in three seconds flat.

From what we could see, at the end of the project, there were double wiring tubes in the walls, one which fed electric wires to all the windows and doors, and the other led to the master panel in the cellar. There, by a simple handling of a lever, the Hagen's could double lock and bolt all doors and windows in the house and keep them all electrically charged.

The Hagen's even had a trap door at the bottom of the stairs leading to the cellar. If the trap door was not properly secured, one would plunge another two and a half meters lower. The trap well was always half full of water. Mr. Hagen explained to me that the water was for his fire pump and hose. They installed multi bolt locks on all doors. The doors were reinforced with steel plate in the middle and had wood on each side so you could not see it. These doors looked like regular doors but were very heavy and each door had six hinges.

We children figured out quite quickly, that these were not normal folk. It was our impression that Hagen and his wife had lots of money but did not want to be seen spending it. They had no car, nor motorcycle - only two bicycles that they rode either late in the evening when it was still daylight, or shortly after sunrise in the morning.

We observed all these mysterious gadgets and became quite suspicious. Mr. and Mrs. Hagen did not realize that we country boys only needed to see the end of a cable or extra hinges on a regular door to conclude that there was more to it than it appeared. We kept all this information to ourselves and only talked about it with Mom and Dad, making sure that we were indoors when we did this. Curiously enough, Mr. Hagen spoke German with a very strong English accent. At one time, I overheard Mr. and Mrs Hagen arguing in Russian. They were completely unaware that I was working in the cellar digging the soil at that moment. Our Mom suspected that they worked as a secret agents for either the west or the east and we left it at that.

Once most of the digging and chiselling was done, the Hagen's did not require our labour any more.

Mysterious things happened while the Hagen's lived at the house. For instance, there was a dead spruce tree at the far end of the property where the creek ran by. An antenna was sometimes visible at the top of this dead spruce, but not always. We never did find out how this antenna extended out of the tree.

One day, my brother Anton saw them driving a Borgward Isabella car in the town of Bernau. He recognized them and memorized their license plate. They must have used their bicycles to pedal to wherever they had their car stashed away or they had another house they operated out of.

Two years later there was a small report printed in the local newspaper about a man by the name of Hagen who was registered as resident in our town. He had been run over by a train on the Salzburg-Munich track some 50 km away. What was he doing walking on a busy railway track? Or was he left there by the KGB or the CIA to be found? Poor Mr. Hagen! What an end he had! We never did hear from Mrs. Hagen again.

The house was sold a year later. But, before it was sold, there seemed to be one or two secret service cars hanging around in their yard. We recognized these cars as their radio antennas were not on the passenger fender up front (the usual spot for them) but rather were in the middle of the roof at the back.

The new owner found that he had a hot water tank that looked like it was properly hooked up, but wasn't. When you pushed hard on a bolt and turned a wing nut, the tank's wrapping would open like a cabinet door. With a combination of four gadgets plus foot pressure, the operation of a fake water valve would open the second compartment. In other words, his hot water tank had absolutely no water in it.

The new owners were Mr. and Mrs. Elkhover, both teachers in the nearby city of Rosenheim. They found that the house was fortified like a bunker and had unrealistic fine wiring leading all over the place, and sometimes to nowhere at all. The most puzzling thing for them was that a lot of the wires led outside. When they tested them, there was nothing at the other end.

This was very mysterious and strange!

CHAPTER 34

THE SPICE LADIES

The "gren weiberl," literally translated the horseradish ladies, arrived in the local area offering merchandise and wares for sale towards the end of October or beginning of November.

The gren weiberl ladies were named after the wonderful horseradish that they sold, both fresh or dried. Dried horseradish lasted a long time. If you were designated to grate some of it into sauces or gravies, guaranteed your eyes would water. The grated flakes were a welcome spice in the otherwise bland food and a hit with the local ladies in their kitchens. Their Russian garlic, and varieties of their dried paprika and red peppers were also favorite items.

These ladies mainly sold herbs and spices, like marjoram, oregano, and lavender. They also made various herbal ointments and blends, specially created to remedy all sorts of pains and aches. These ointments were sold in tiny, delicate, hand blown glass containers with dainty cherry wood stoppers. Some of the most popular ointments were arnica and gentian roots. Arnica is a yellow-orangey mountain flower that, when preserved in alcohol, was commonly used as an antiseptic medicine that was applied to wounds. Gentian roots, also preserved in alcohol, was used similarly to arnica.

Lavender soap bars were quite expensive and were much sought after by their customers, as were the variety of garden seed for the upcoming planting season. They had a great selection of beautiful knitted tuques, mittens, men's sweaters and extra fancy ones for the girls and ladies with elaborate patterns of flowers and braided wool. They also had a wide selection of finely woven baskets, which had a variety of uses.

The leader of the group, Mila, was a likeable, lively lady in her early forties, of average height, with sparkling blue eyes and blond curly hair. She and her girls all wore very colorful head scarves that were common to the area where they came from.

Mila was slightly on the chubby side, very chatty and polite. She told flourishing stories that kept her clients spellbound while they were shopping from her wares. Her stories were always happy and humorous which made her clients linger for a while longer thus buying a few extra things. Mila's happy stories were also welcomed as the war years brought a lot of misery to their region.

One of Mila's stories was about a well to do farmer's widow, Mrs. Lisa Hakel, whose husband had died in 1941 while fighting on the western front. Mrs. Hakel thought that she had lost her locket pendant and chain that she had received from her grandmother Therese on her tenth birthday. This had been very dear to her as it had a special engraving on it and she considered it to be her good luck charm. The engraving was of Saint Therese with the number 1881 on it. Mrs. Hakel considered the number one and number eight to be very, very lucky numbers.

This was October 1945. All that Mrs. Hakel could remember was that she had been wearing the locket before she went to the outhouse a week earlier. She searched and searched everywhere intensively, but it was all in vain. She convinced herself that the chain must have broken and slipped down into the waste tank of the outhouse.

After a considerable length of time Mrs. Hakel decided to offer a reward of a hundred German Marks to anyone who recovered her locket from the waste tank. This was considered a large sum of money in those days. She made an arrangement with the local priest, Father Nikolas Feder, by giving him a fair donation to his church in return for him to attach the "Notice of Request" on church bulletin boards throughout the neighboring communities in the area. Father Nikolas did not waste any time. He bicycled all over the area for the next two or three days until all the bulletin boards had the notice of the reward for the lost locket and chain.

Some sarcastic and forked tongued villagers made nasty comments and suggested that Mrs. Hakel wanted to have her waste tank cleaned out for free! These rumors travelled throughout the area.

After a week, when nobody else came forward, a daredevil farm worker showed up and applied for the chance to find the lost locket and chain, and thereby claim the reward.

He introduced himself as Wolfgang Hirsch. He was a tall, blond, blue eyed, man with a muscular built body, and of similar age as Mrs. Hakel. He lived and worked at a farm eighteen kilometers away. Wolfgang was an ex-paratrooper. He was a quiet fellow and never bragged about his military experiences. Sadly, he had lost his home and family near Leipzig, during the Russian advance, and had now started a new life as a farm worker. Wolfgang contemplated that he would collect the reward within two days and it was his dream that he would buy himself a genuine Swiss Omega pocket watch with that money, similar to the one that his parents had had in Leipzig, but had been destroyed along with the family home during the bombing.

The following Sunday, on his day off, Wolfgang worked very hard and proceeded to empty the tank bucket by bucket, wheelbarrow by wheelbarrow. From sunrise to sunset, he worked in the heavy rain, wind and sleet, which made his job twice as difficult.

He carefully spread the contents of the tank out on an empty potato field, where it would be ploughed under by the horse and plough team the following week, as it was already late fall. As he worked, he kept a vigilant eye out for the chain and locket. After the third Sunday of hard work, he finally completed the job. He was very disappointed that he had not found what he so carefully had looked for. To make matters worse, the villagers' rumors intensified and got even nastier.

Luckily, a few weeks later, Mrs. Hakel finally found her locket in the back of the bottom drawer of her night table. She struggled with her conscience for a few days and, in her daily prayers, asked St. Anthony for advice. She finally came to the conclusion to admit her mistake, tell the truth and pay Wolfgang his reward.

Some lazy bone villagers were now very jealous of Wolfgang's reward, saying that he had not really worked that hard. Mrs. Hakel and Wolfgang became friendlier and were seen together the following spring and summer at the local festivals, and at some dances as well. Another eight months passed, when Father Nikolas Feder nailed up the announcement of the upcoming marriage of Mr. Wolfgang Hirsch and Mrs. Lisa Hakel on the church's announcement board.

Wolfgang got his Swiss Omega pocket watch capable of producing an exquisite sounding "ding-dong" chime. He bought himself a trumpet and then played in the local village music band. Lisa and Wolfgang adopted two war orphan children Eva, seven years old and Tony who was nine. They showered these quiet children with much love.

Mila travelled with her daughter Anya, who was a very pretty twenty-two year old. She was taller than her mother, with her long blond hair braided into one ponytail that lay past her shoulders. Anya also had blue eyes like her Mother and younger sister Marja. Marja was twenty and almost identical to her older sister, except that she sported two pigtails with her blonde shoulder length hair. The fourth lady in the team was Mila's niece Tatina. She was a fiery nineteen year old, with her long black hair braided in two pigtails that almost reached her waist, dark vivid eyes, and the most perfectly formed generous red lips - which made every man think of how wonderful it would be to be kissed by them.

They all had a healthy colored complexion from being outside so much, but Tatina's skin was almost hazel, matching her eyes. Most likely she had some gypsy blood in her veins. The girls were all slim and perfectly shaped. As they went from village to village, two of the girls pulled a fair sized hickory wagon. It had metal-rimmed wooden wheels with a rounded canvas top to protect their belongings and wares from the elements. The "graxen," (backpack baskets), were stacked into each other and were attached at the rear of the cart. The remaining two girls walked behind and they would alternate with the girls pulling the wagon every so often, until they arrived at a cluster of houses or farms where they could sell their wears. The girls all loved singing, so as they walked along, they sang many of the "happy wanderer" songs popular in those days.

When they arrived at a village, Mila remained with her wagon and one set of the backpack baskets, while the three girls went off to the nearby farms that they could reach within a days walk, carrying their baskets. Farmers on their way home from the flourmill, blacksmith or sawmill with their horses and wagons, were delighted to offer these girls a ride to their destination or return from it.

Yes, word spread well ahead of the spice ladies' arrival at the village center, so as soon as Mila was set up for commerce, folks were already waiting for them. They stood around her wagon with lots of patience while she set up her display and were very curious to see what new products were available that year.

On their journeys, Mila was carefully gathering information about well to do farmers or mill owners with sons that could be eligible husbands for her girls. These were tough times as there was actually a shortage of men everywhere because the world war claimed too many men - some were missing in action, others killed or interned in the prisoner of war camps.

Although people had very little money, they were very happy to acquire something special for themselves and their family. All day long, customers were buying and bartering. Mila had a way to make all her customers feel good - with a twinkle in her eye she slipped many poorer customers an extra envelope of seeds, paprika, oregano or marjoram and so on, into their shopping wicker basket.

Naturally, Mila was very much aware who were the wives of the wealthier farmers or sawmill owners and they certainly drove a hard bargain. She was familiar with their ways of doing business and with a smiling face, she succeeded in selling them double or triple the amount of items they had originally planned to buy, and also a few more of the expensive items, like the lavender soap, elk horn buttons, etc. She was very quick and observed every signal on the customers face and body language. After every sale, Mila would bow and thank each and every customer with sincere eye contact and a smile. In a way, she made all her customers feel elated and good. They always went away feeling that they had gotten a very good deal from her.

In some small villages, there were only a few houses surrounding the church. If many homes and farms were in clusters within a radius of seven kilometers, Mila would leave her wagon with the local priest, while all four of the team made their rounds with their merchandise in the backpack baskets. The priest, Father Martin in turn would lock the wagon for safe keeping in the local church until Mila and the girls arrived back from their selling spree. He would be rewarded with a small dried bouquet of lavender which he appreciated very much and used the opportunity to bless Mila and the girls and their wagon.

On their journeys they travelled on gravel roads, as in those days there were no paved roads in this area. They made good use of their canvas tent for overnight shelter, as they could not afford a room in a guesthouse. Sometimes, they were invited by some generous farmers to set up their tent under the big roof of the hay barn, and sometimes, if there was space available, they were offered a room for one night and occasionally a hot meal with it. A warm and cozy spot by the Kachel Ofen (tile oven) would entice Mila to bring out her guitar and Anja her accordion, and they would provide some wonderful music and everyone else sang along. At ten o'clock at night sharp, the girls would retire to their beds and be up and ready at seven in the morning to continue their journey.

Mila and her girls were always spotlessly clean and fresh looking. They took advantage of convenient creeks, wells and those usual fountain spouts in front of the farm houses, where a hollowed out log acted as a water trough for fresh water that was coming in through a pipe and at the other end a drain pipe would take the excess water away. The ladies were very quick in stripping down and washing themselves even if it was very cold. Two of the girls would hold up a canvas blanket for privacy, while the other two were busy lathering, washing, rinsing and drying. They took turns doing this.

They walked from village to village continuing their journey west. Finally, about thirty-five kilometers past our village, they were sold out. Mila sold their hickory wagon, the canvass tent and their unique graxen to alpine farmers who appreciated these items and valued them highly.

The time had arrived for Mila and the girls to go home. They acquired train tickets and went via Rosenheim, Traunstein and Passau. It took them four days to get to their waiting families back home. The following year, in 1948, Anja married a handsome young farmer near Traunstein. Mila kept her customers updated on her yearly journeys. She was very proud that she was a happy Grandma of a baby boy called Andreas.

As time went by, Mila's girls were all married and she traveled with new girls that she claimed were her nieces. In 1954, Mila made her last journey because she purchased a business in her hometown and made it quite successful. She could now afford a Volkswagen beetle car and she made sure she visited her daughters and grandchildren regularly.

Hardship was very widespread at the end of the Second World War in Germany.

This provided unlimited "adventures" in which adults and children had to use all their wits to make daily life a little bit better than what the circumstances actually were. A small amount of good will touched many!

Willi Meyer lives in Langley with his wife Frances. They both like to go fishing and camping in beautiful British Columbia and entertain their Grandsons and their friends.

Made in the USA
Middletown, DE
22 July 2017